OpenOffice 3.4
Volume II: Calc

quantum scientific publishing

OpenOffice 3.4
Volume II: Calc

CHRISTOPHER N. CAIN

RILEY W. WALKER

quantum scientific publishing

OpenOffice 3.4
Volume II: Calc

ISBN-13: 978-1480224346
ISBN-10: 1480224340

Published by quantum scientific publishing

Pittsburgh, PA | Copyright © 2012

All rights reserved. Permission in writing must be obtained from the publisher before any part of this work may be reproduced or transmitted in any form, including photocopying and recording.

OpenOffice and the OpenOffice logo are trademarks or registered trademarks of The Apache Software Foundation and/or its affiliates.

Cover design by Scott Sheariss

Unit One

Section 1.1 – Introduction to OpenOffice Calc   2

Section 1.2 – Using a Spreadsheet   4

Section 1.3 – Saving a Spreadsheet   8

Section 1.4 – Changing Cell Properties   11

Section 1.5 – Changing Spreadsheet Margins   17

Section 1.6 – Using Drag and Drop   20

Section 1.7 – Using Copy and Cut   22

Section 1.8 – Adding and Removing Columns and Rows   25

Section 1.9 – Hiding and Revealing Columns and Rows   28

Section 1.10 – Hiding Cell Contents   32

Section 1.11 – Freezing and Unfreezing Panes   35

Section 1.12 – Using Split Screen and the Multiple Page Feature   38

Section 1.13 – Using the Merge and Center Button   41

Section 1.14 – Adding Clip Art to a Spreadsheet   44

Section 1.15 – Searching for Data in a Spreadsheet   49

Unit Two

Section 2.1 – Calculating Data   54

Section 2.2 – Naming Groups of Data   56

Section 2.3 – Creating Formulas   60

Section 2.4 – Different Types of Operators   62

Section 2.5 – Using the Detective Tool   64

Section 2.6 – Spreadsheet Auditing   68

Section 2.7 – Adding Subtotals to a Spreadsheet   70

Section 2.8 – Adding a Chart to a Spreadsheet   74

Section 2.9 – Entering Data into Multiple Spreadsheets   80

Section 2.10 – Using Screen Filters to Limit Data   83

Section 2.11 – Creating a Custom Filter   86

Section 2.12 – Working With Advanced Filters   91

Section 2.13 – Getting Running Totals   96

Section 2.14 – Improving Accuracy of Spreadsheets   98

Section 2.15 – Sorting Data   101

Unit Three

- Section 3.1 – Changing the Appearance of a Document   108
- Section 3.2 – Types of Tools on the Formatting Toolbar   111
- Section 3.3 – Using Font Color and Size Control Tools   114
- Section 3.4 – Using the Borders Button   117
- Section 3.5 – Using the Fill Button   121
- Section 3.6 – Exporting Spreadsheets to a PDF   125
- Section 3.7 – Applying Formatting to Numbers   132
- Section 3.8 – Adding Date and Time   135
- Section 3.9 – Using Headers and Footers   137
- Section 3.10 – Formatting Cells Using Conditional Formatting   141
- Section 3.11 – Creating a Customized Conditional Formatting Style   145
- Section 3.12 – Editing Conditional Formatting Styles   151
- Section 3.13 – Positioning Data on a Printout   155
- Section 3.14 – Defining Print Area   160
- Section 3.15 – Printing Ranges of Cells   163

Appendix

- OpenOffice Volume II: Calc Answer Key   170

Unit One

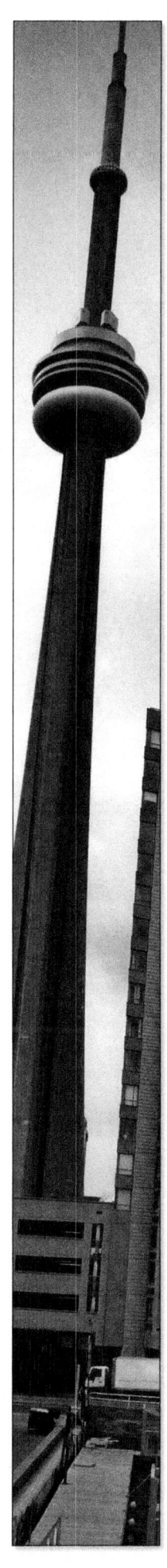

Section 1.1 – Introduction to OpenOffice Calc   2

Section 1.2 – Using a Spreadsheet   4

Section 1.3 – Saving a Spreadsheet   8

Section 1.4 – Changing Cell Properties   11

Section 1.5 – Changing Spreadsheet Margins   17

Section 1.6 – Using Drag and Drop   20

Section 1.7 – Using Copy and Cut   22

Section 1.8 – Adding and Removing Columns and Rows   25

Section 1.9 – Hiding and Revealing Columns and Rows   28

Section 1.10 – Hiding Cell Contents   32

Section 1.11 – Freezing and Unfreezing Panes   35

Section 1.12 – Using Split Screen and the Multiple Page Feature   38

Section 1.13 – Using the Merge and Center Button   41

Section 1.14 – Adding ClipArt to a Spreadsheet   44

Section 1.15 – Searching for Data in a Spreadsheet   49

Section 1.1 – Introduction to OpenOffice Calc

Section Objective:

- Learn how to begin using OpenOffice Calc.

Introduction

Welcome to OpenOffice Calc. Calc is a free and powerful spreadsheet tool, and is just one of six applications found within the Apache OpenOffice Suite 3.4. If not already installed, download the latest version of the Apache OpenOffice Suite from the www.openoffice.org website. When the page loads, click "I want to download OpenOffice" to be directed to the download page. Follow the instructions to complete the download.

This book begins by introducing the basic features and layout of Calc, and then progresses to more complex functions and operations. At the end of each section, there are questions meant to test readers' understanding of the application. Use these questions, as well as the steps provided in this book, to learn many different tasks which can be accomplished in OpenOffice Calc.

Features in OpenOffice Calc

OpenOffice Calc combines the column/row layout of traditional paper spreadsheets with powerful tools that the user can use for data calculation, analysis, and formatting. Calc, like most applications has its own terminology, but once learned, a user can easily understand the features and tools provided by the application. The following terms will help users when starting out in Calc.

- **Cell** – The intersection of a column and row. All information inserted into the application will be stored in cells.

- **Cell Pointer** – The cell pointer is similar to Writer's insertion point. It selects or marks the current cell. The Calc pointer changes shape depending on location and corresponding function.

- **Cell Reference** – A cell reference is an address, consisting of the column and row IDs, of a specific cell. The current cell position is displayed in the top left-hand corner of the spreadsheet.

- **Column** – A column is a vertical group of cells within a spreadsheet.

- **Formula** – A formula is a set of instructions that perform a calculation based on numbers entered in the cell or numbers entered in multiple cells. All formulas begin with the equal sign [=].

- **Function** – A pre-programmed formula. The function performs the calculation based on the cells referenced in the function. All functions begin with the equal sign [=].

- **Range** – A range is a group of cells. Ranges can be selected by clicking and dragging over the cells.

- **Row** – A row is a horizontal group of cells within a spreadsheet.

- **Value** – A number that can be used in a Calc calculation.

- **Spreadsheet** - A single sheet within a spreadsheet document.. A spreadsheet can contain data, charts, or both. Several spreadsheets can be combined together which is helpful when working on a project with multiple components.

Growth & Assessment

1. What is a cell in OpenOffice Calc?

2. Columns are horizontal groups of cells within a spreadsheet.

    a. TRUE

    b. FALSE

3. What is a spreadsheet?

4. What do all formulas begin with?

Section 1.2 – Using a Spreadsheet

Section Objectives:

- Learn how to create a new spreadsheet.
- Learn how to enter data into a spreadsheet.

Creating a New Spreadsheet in Calc

OpenOffice Calc refers to its files as **Spreadsheet Documents**. New When a new spreadsheet document is created, by default it opens with three spreadsheets for the user to work with. **Spreadsheets** can be added or deleted at any time. This section covers the steps necessary to create a new spreadsheet and explains how users can enter data into the application once the spreadsheet is set up.

When OpenOffice Calc is first opened, a new blank spreadsheet documents will appear on the screen. As mentioned above, it contains three blank spreadsheets which are ready for use, and is formatted to Calc's default settings.

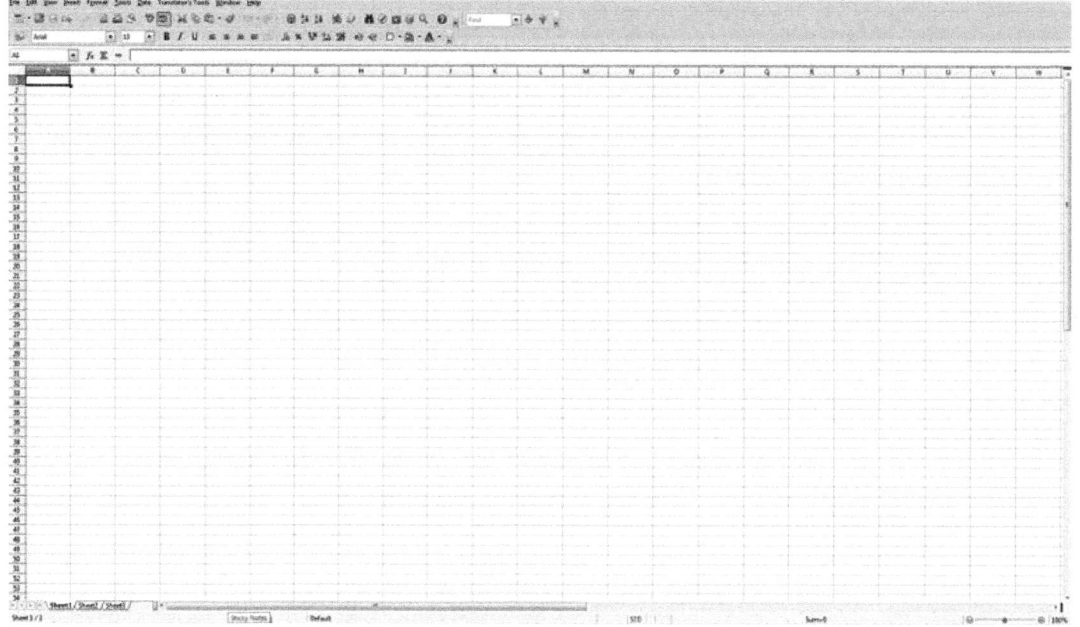

Figure 1

If a new spreadsheet is needed, and the application had just been used or its format has been altered, the following steps outline how users can create a new blank spreadsheet without having to close and reopen the application.

Step 1: Click **File** on the Menu Bar.

Step 2: From the File drop-down menu, click **New** and then select **Spreadsheet**.

   Note – A new spreadsheet can also be created by using the keyboard short "**CTRL + N**."

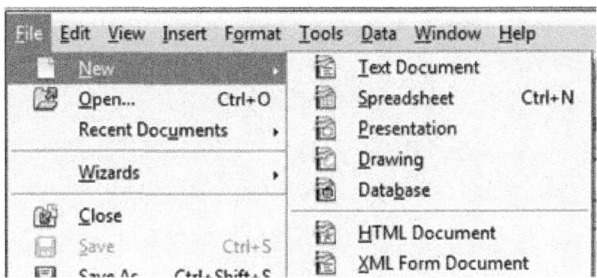

Figure 2

Entering Data into a Spreadsheet

Once a new spreadsheet has been created, users can start entering data into it. The following steps will explain how to enter text and numerical values into the cells of OpenOffice Calc.

Entering Text into the Cells

Step 1: Select cell **A1** in the top-left of the spreadsheet.

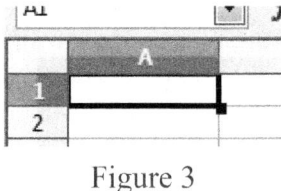

Figure 3

Step 2: Type a word into the cell.

Step 3: Press **ENTER** or **TAB** to accept the text. Calc will automatically left-align the text entered.

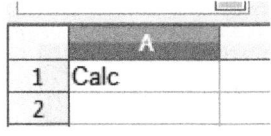

Figure 4

Entering Numerical Values into the Cells

Note – Numerical cells can be used for calculations and functions. A numerical cell may contain numbers, a decimal point (.), plus (+) or minus (−) signs, and currency ($).

Step 1: Select the cell **B1**.

Step 2: Type a number into the cell.

Step 3: To accept the numerical value, press **ENTER** or **TAB**. Calc will automatically right-align numerical values.

Note – Within each cell, all text will be left-aligned and all numerical values will be right-aligned.

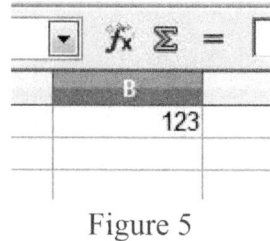

Figure 5

Formatting Cells for Text

In Calc, when cells are formatted for text, all cell contents—letters, numerals, and alphanumerical combinations—are treated as text. Information is displayed exactly as it is entered. The following steps outline how this is done.

Step 1: Select cell **C2** and click **Format** on the Menu Bar.

Step 2: From the Format menu, click **Cells**…. The **Format Cells** dialog box appears.

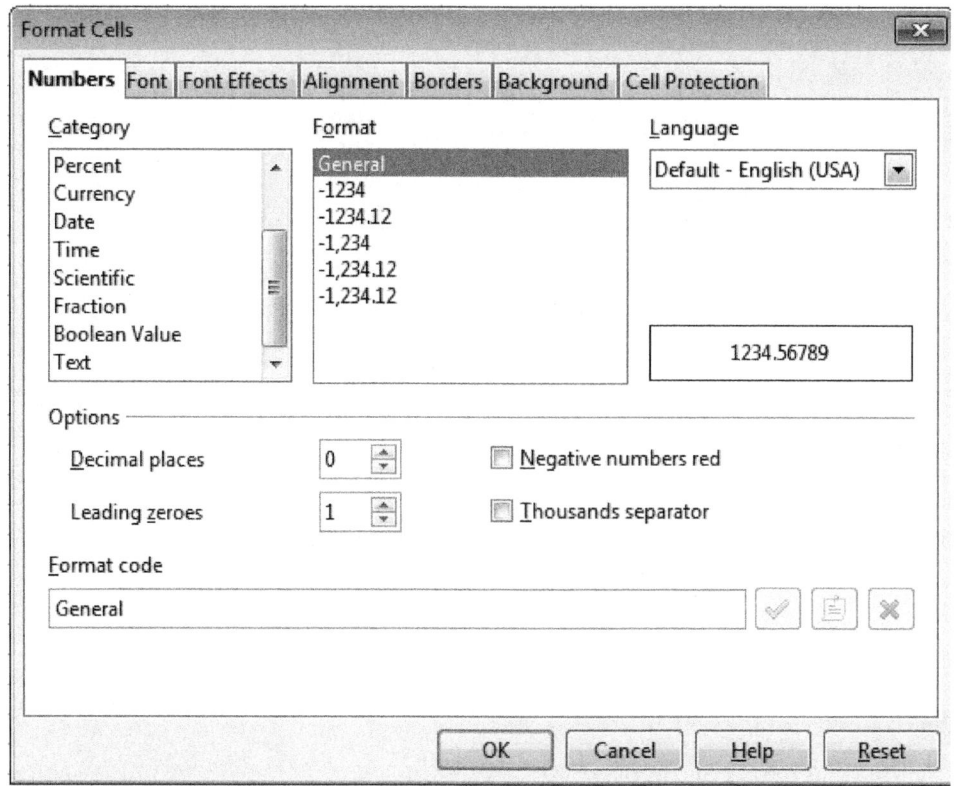

Figure 6

6

Step 3: Select the **Number** tab if it is not already selected.

Step 4: From the **Category** scroll list, select **Text**.

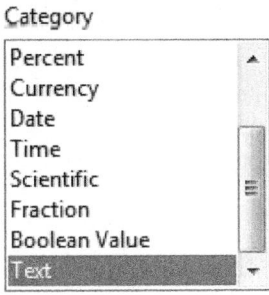

Figure 7

Step 5: Click **OK**.

Growth & Assessment

1. What is the keyboard shortcut to open a new spreadsheet?

2. What is the name of the option users would select when opening a new spreadsheet, all while keeping the application open?

3. When a cell is formatted for text, all letters, numerals, and alphanumerical combinations within that cell are treated as text.

    a. TRUE

    b. FALSE

7

Section 1.3 – Saving a Spreadsheet

Section Objective:

- Learn how to save a spreadsheet.

Saving a Spreadsheet in Calc

In OpenOffice Calc, the **Save** and **Save As** commands are located within the **File** menu on the Menu Bar. If a spreadsheet has never been saved before, both selections (**Save** and **Save As**) will take the user to the **Save As** dialog box. The **Save As** dialog box allows the user to select a particular file format when saving. The following steps outline how saving a spreadsheet is done.

Step 1: Create a new Calc Spreadsheet.

Step 2: Click **File**, located in the Menu Bar.

Step 3: If the document has already been saved to a particular folder, select **Save** to update the spreadsheet from the previously saved version. If not, selecting **Save** or **Save As**, will open the **Save As** dialog box.

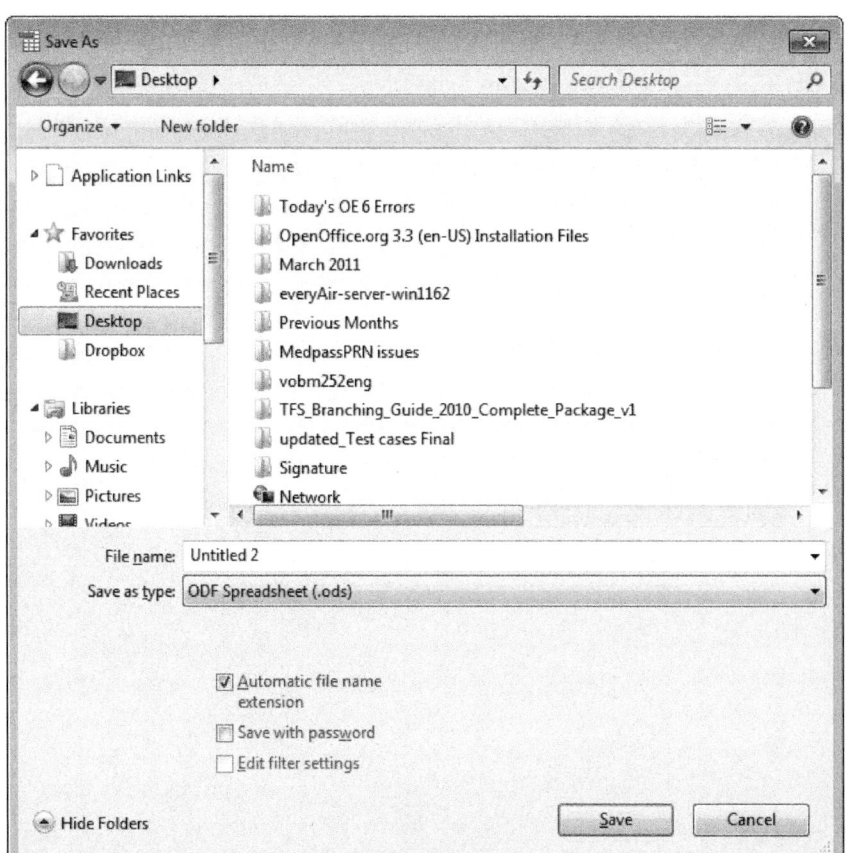

Figure 1

Step 4: From the **Save As** dialog box, Calc allows the user choose the location in which the spreadsheet will be saved. Select the preferred file.

Step 4: In the **File Name** textbox, type a file name. Once a file name is chosen, click **Save**. Once the spreadsheet is saved, the name of the spreadsheet will be visible in the title bar located along the top of the application window.

Figure 2

Note – The keyboard shortcut **CTRL + S** will automatically save the document if it has been saved previously. If not, this shortcut will open the **Save As** dialog box.

Saving a Calc Spreadsheet as a Microsoft Excel File

All files are saved with a particular file extension. A file extension is simply the ending of the named file. Also, the file extension is specific to the program and application from which the field was created. The default file format for Calc is ".ods" (an open source format), but the application allows the user to save the spreadsheet in the ".xls" format used in Excel 97-2003. Saving Calc spreadsheets in the Excel 97-2003 file format allows the spreadsheet to also be edited in Microsoft Excel. Follow these steps to save in the ".xls" format.

Step 1: Click **File**, located on the Menu Bar.

Step 2: From the File menu, select **Save As**. The **Save As** dialog box will appear.

Step 3: Open the **Save as type:** drop-down menu and select **Microsoft Excel 97/2000/XP (.xls)**.

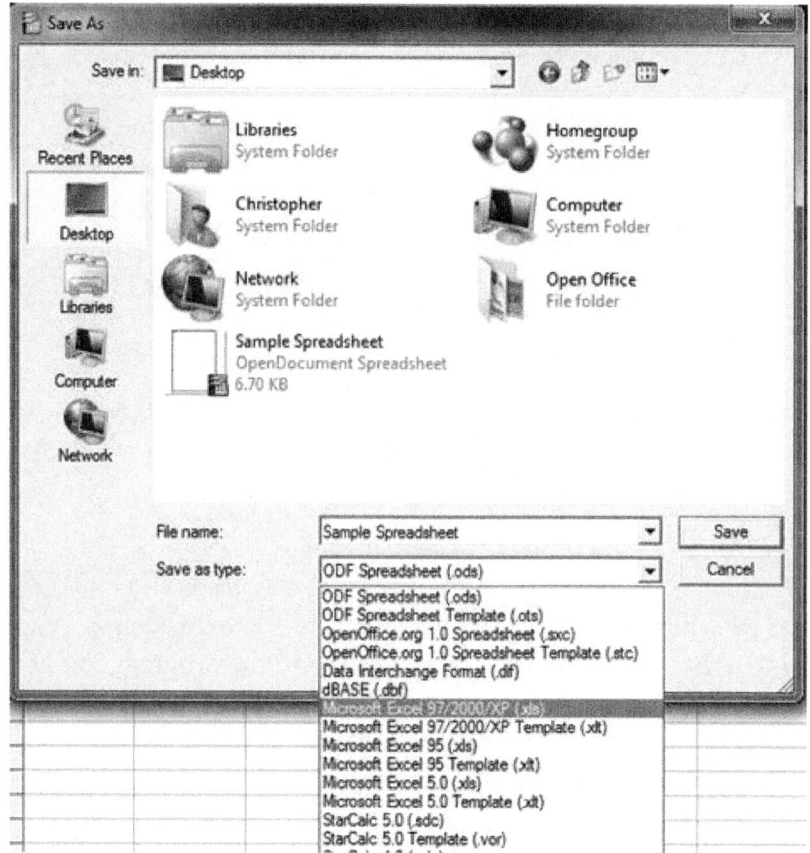

Figure 3

Step 4: Once the file extension has changed from ".ods" to ".xls," click **Save**.

Growth & Assessment

1. What is the standard file extension used for OpenOffice files?

2. Users are able to save a Calc spreadsheet as a Microsoft Excel File, ".xls"?

    a. TRUE

    b. FALSE

3. What is the keyboard shortcut to save a document?

4. What is the purpose of the **Save As** dialog box?

Section 1.4 – Changing Cell Properties

Section Objective:

- Learn how to change cell properties with styles.

Using Styles to Change Cell Properties

OpenOffice Calc offers styles that can be applied to elements within the spreadsheet. Styles are a set of formats that allow the user to quickly change the appearance of a spreadsheet. Styles help with consistency and save the user time when formatting large spreadsheet documents that contain multiple spreadsheets.

Calc offers two different types of preset styles: **Cell Styles** and **Page Styles**. Both of these styles are described below.

- **Cell Style** – This style is used for formatting cells (the intersections of the rows and columns). The style includes fonts, boarders, cell background, number formats (currency, date, etc…), alignment, and cell protection (protects the cells from certain types of editing).

- **Page Style** – This style is used for the spreadsheets in Calc. Only one style can be applied to a spreadsheet even if it is multiple pages long. The style includes headers and footers, boarders and backgrounds, and margins. The other formats bundled in this style apply to the spreadsheet when it is ready to print. Some of these printing formats affect the page size and the orientation of the spreadsheet.

Calc not only provides the two options above, but also allows the user to create custom styles. This feature allows the user to not only create a name for the new style, but also define the formatting characteristics, and select additional options that give the user even more control over the look of the spreadsheet. The following steps explain how to do this in OpenOffice Calc.

Step 1: Create a new spreadsheet in Calc.

Step 2: Click **Format** located on the Menu Bar.

Step 3: From the Format menu, select **Styles and Formatting**. The **Styles and Formatting** dialog box will appear.

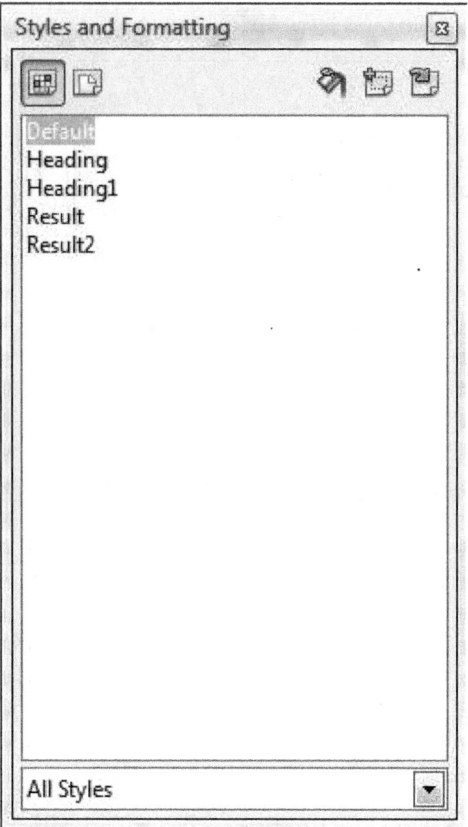

Figure 1

Note – The keyboard shortcut **F11** will open the **Styles and Formatting** dialog box.

Step 4: Select the **Cell Styles** icon or the **Page Styles** icon at the top of the **Styles and Formatting** dialog box to identify which type of style is desired.

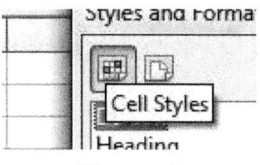

Figure 2

Step 5: Right-click anywhere within the **Styles and Formatting** dialog box and select **New…** from the quick menu.

12

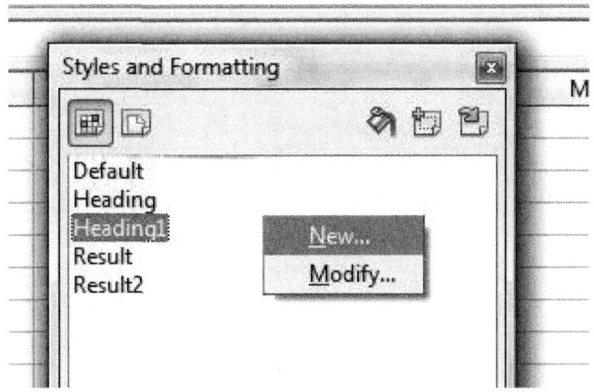

Figure 3

Step 6: The **Cell Style** or **Page Style** dialog box will appear, depending on what was selected in **Step 4**. Here, Calc allows users to name the new style. Type in a file name and click **OK**.

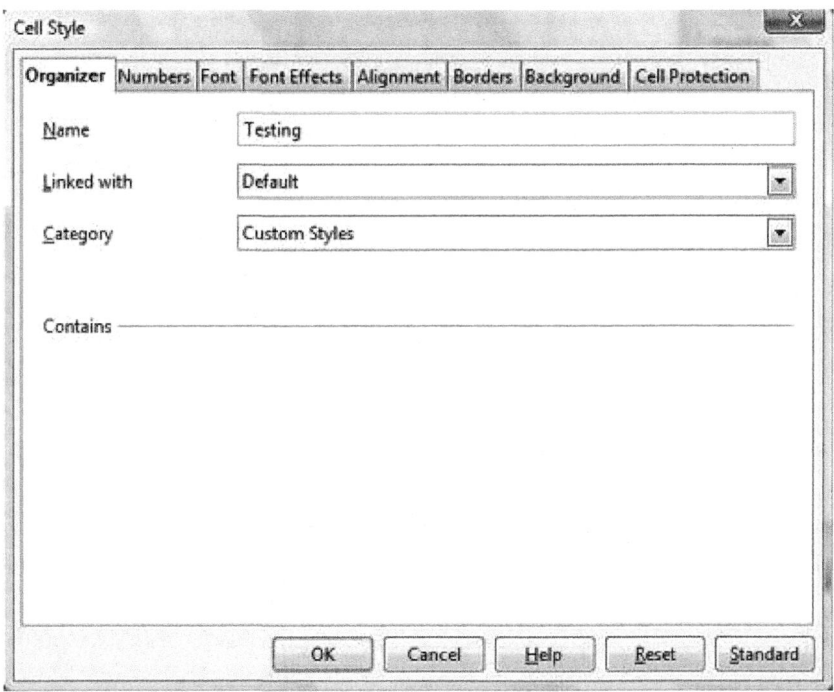

Figure 4

Step 7: Once **OK** has been clicked, the new style will be added to the **Styles and Formatting** window.

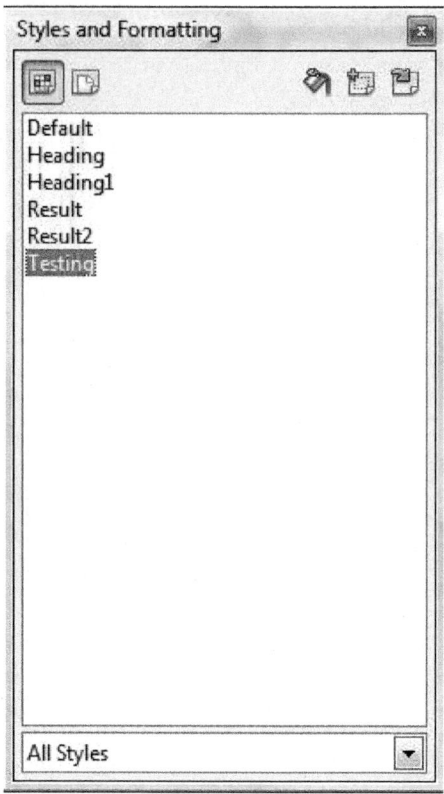

Figure 5

Step 8: Right-click on the newly created style and select **Modify…**.

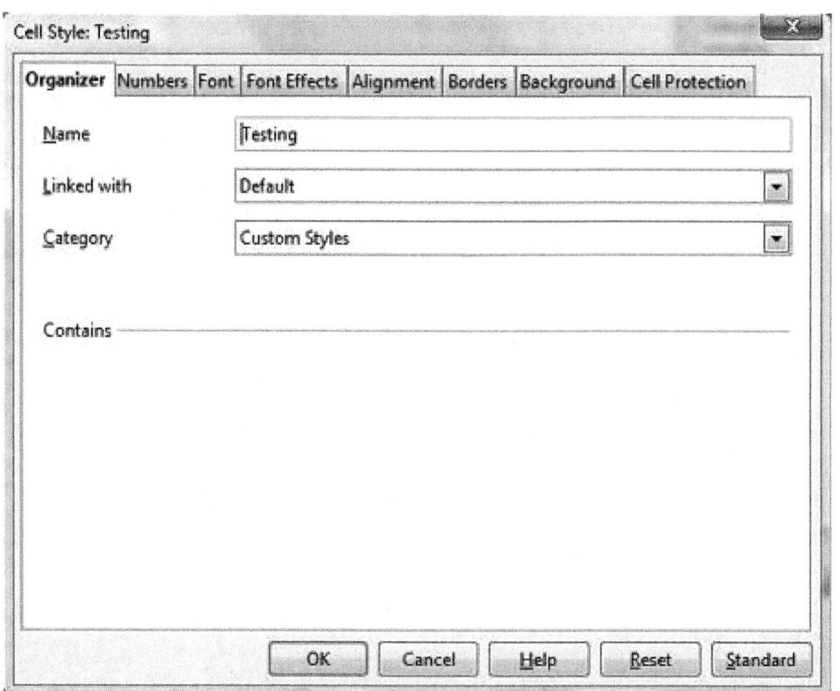

Figure 6

Up to this point, the two types of styles (**Cell Styles** and **Page Styles**) have required the same steps. At this point, Calc allows users to modify various aspects of the new style. Depending on which style icon was selected in **Step 4**, users will be presented with different style modification options. Below, the steps for making both types of modifications are outlined.

Modifying a New Cell Style

Step 1: After right-clicking on the newly created style in **Step 8**, the **Cell Style** dialog box will appear.

Step 2: Click the **Font** tab located at the top of the window. In the **Font** portion of the dialog box, Calc allows the user to modify the font, font size, and typeface of the text entered into the cells. The other tabs located at the top of the window allow the user to modify borders, cell background, number formats, alignment, and cell protection settings of the cells, for the new style. Once these have been selected, click **OK**.

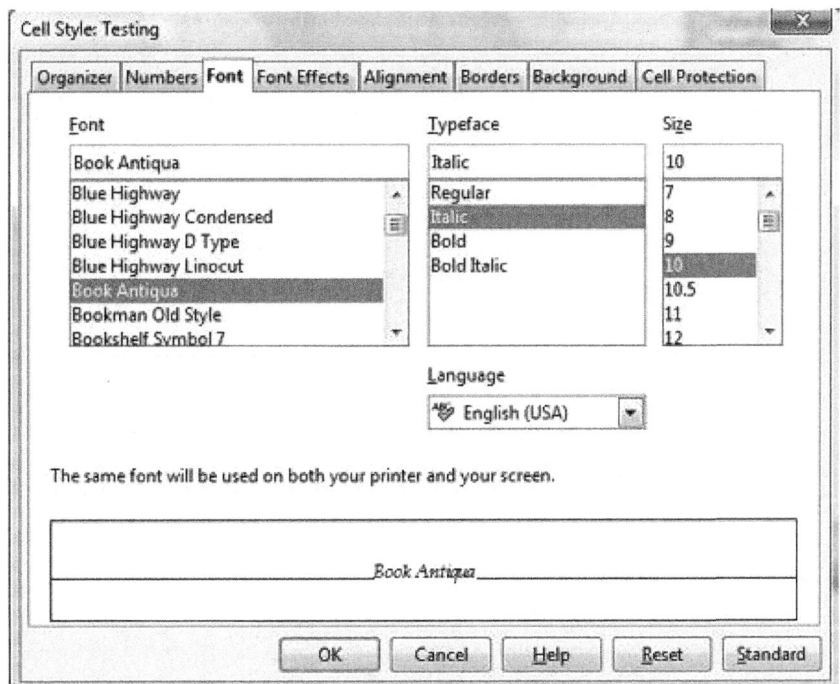

Figure 7

Modifying a New Page Style

Step 1: After right-clicking on the newly created style in **Step 8**, the **Page Style** dialog box will appear.

Step 2: Click the **Page** tab located at the top of the window. In the Page portion of the dialog box, Calc allows the user to modify the page format, the margins, and the layout settings for when the spreadsheets are ready to be printed. The other tabs located at the top of the window allow the user to modify borders, the background, and the headers and footers for the new style. Once these have been selected, click **OK**.

Growth & Assessment

1. What are the two different types of preset styles?

2. The Page Style formats are applied to the whole spreadsheet.

    a. TRUE

    b. FALSE

3. What kinds of items are able to be formatted in the **Font** portion of the **Cell Style** dialog box?

4. What is the keyboard shortcut used to open the Styles and Formatting dialog box?

Section 1.5 – Changing Spreadsheet Margins

Section Objective:

- Learn how to change spreadsheet margins.

Changing Spreadsheet Margins

The margins in OpenOffice Calc are the blank borders that go around the outside of a spreadsheet. Usually, no text and/or graphics are inserted into the margin area other than page numbers, headers and footers. Calc allows users to adjust the margins of a spreadsheet to a preferred width. This is a helpful feature when graphics such as pie charts, histograms, and other visuals are inserted into a spreadsheet because these graphics need to be displayed in an organized way, and without adjusting the margins, these visuals may not fit properly if using the default settings.

Steps for Adjusting the Spreadsheet Margins

Note – The default margins in Calc are **.79** inches for all four margins.

Step 1: Create a new Calc spreadsheet.

Step 2: Click **Format**, located on the Menu Bar, to expand the drop-down menu.

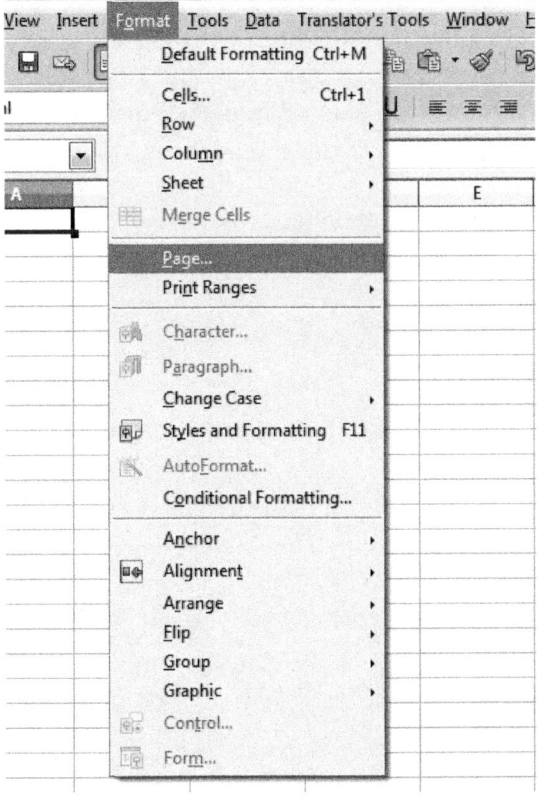

Figure 1

Step 3: From the drop-down menu, click **Page…**, which will cause the **Page Style: Default** window to appear.

Step 4: Select the **Page** tab. This will cause the **Page Subscreen** to appear.

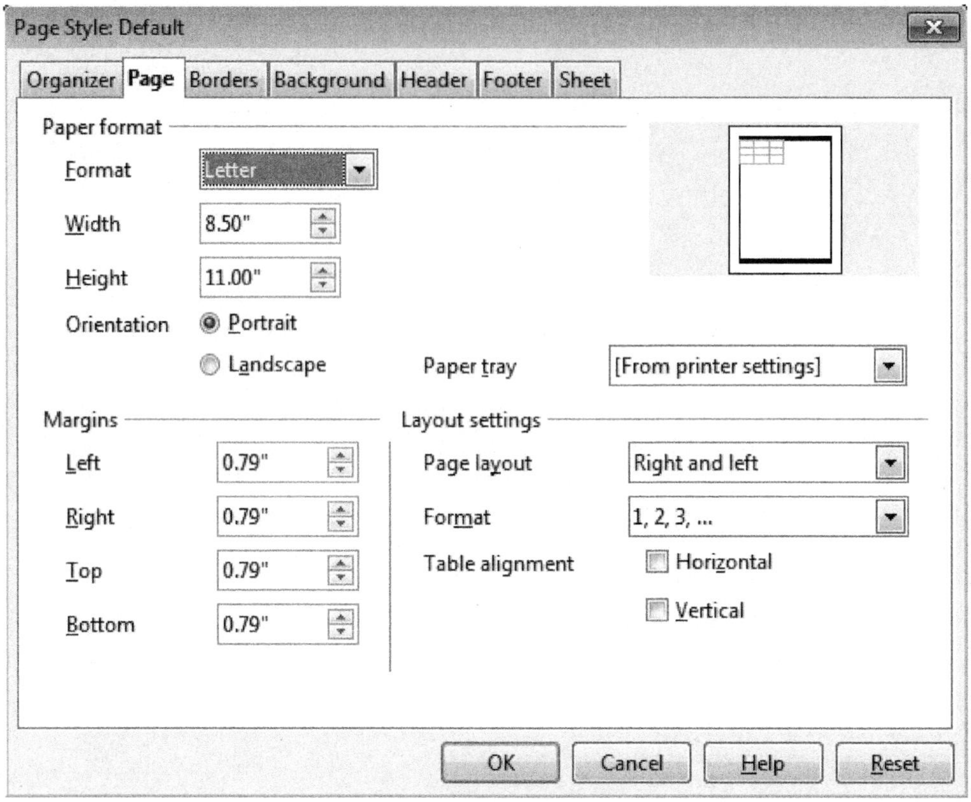

Figure 2

Step 5: In the bottom left of the window there will be four textboxes where the user can enter the margins for the top, bottom, left, and right sides of the spreadsheet. Once the desired amount has been entered into each margin textbox, click **OK**. This will apply the new margin width to the spreadsheet.

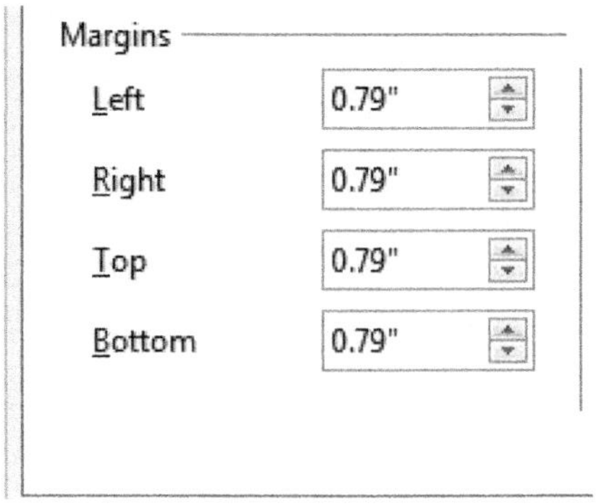

Figure 3

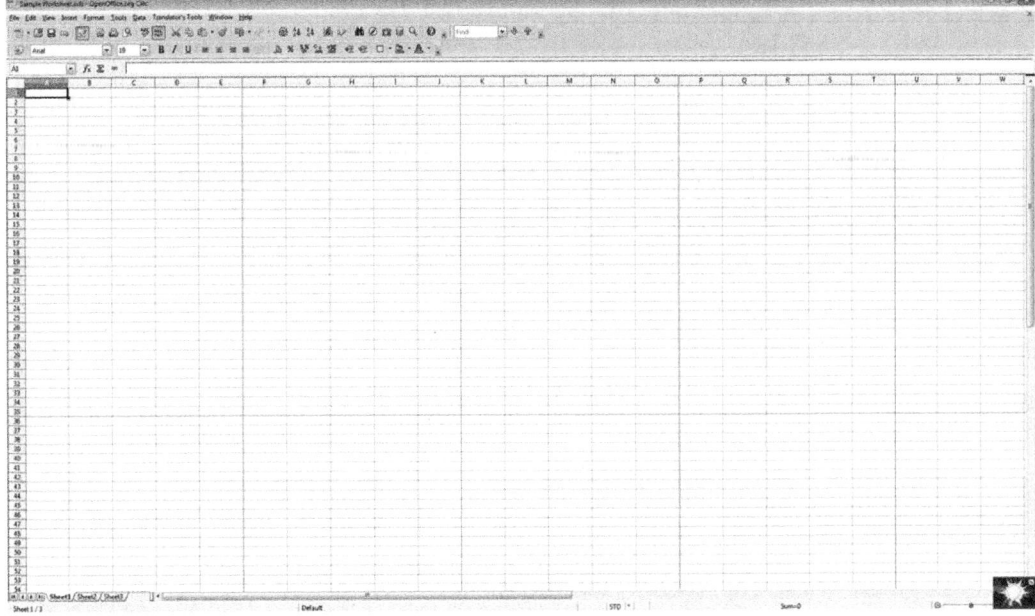

Figure 4

After applying the new margins to the spreadsheet it is important to scroll through the document's pages to make sure the new margins didn't distort any of the elements within it. Also, Calc displays dark lines on the spreadsheet which can be used to identify which cells will be included in a single printable page.

Growth & Assessment

1. What are the default margins in Calc?

2. What are margins?

3. Calc displays dark lines on the spreadsheet to help identify which cells will be included in a single printable page.

    a. TRUE

    b. FALSE

Section 1.6 – Using Drag and Drop

Section Objective:

- Learn how to move data in a spreadsheet using drag and drop.

The Drag and Drop Method

OpenOffice Calc allows users to move entered data from one cell to another by using the drag and drop method. This method allows the user to easily transfer text by simply dragging a cell from its original location and dropping it to its new location. The following steps outline how this task is done.

Step 1: Create a new Calc spreadsheet and enter text into one cell. After entering the text, select the cell.

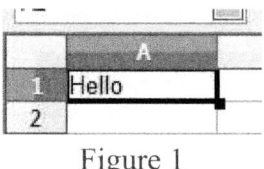

Figure 1

Step 2: Place the cursor anywhere within the highlighted cell.

Step 3: Click and hold the left mouse button.

Step 4: Drag the cell to another cell within a spreadsheet. An outline of the cell being moved, will appear over its new location.

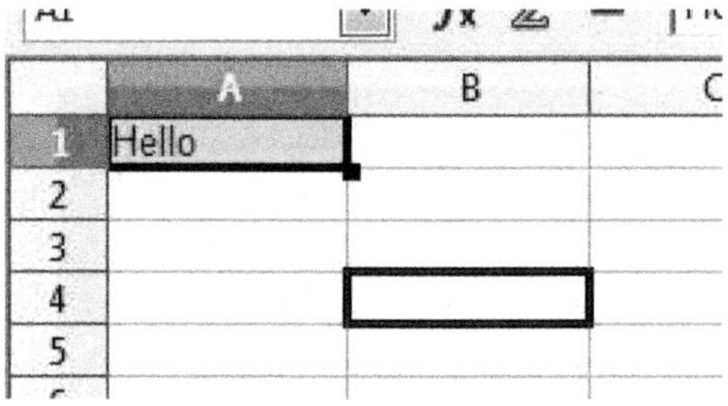

Figure 2

Step 5: Once the outline of the cell is positioned over its new location, release the left mouse button to drop the cell. This will cause the text entered into the original cell to move to the new cell location. If there is data already in the destination cell, the new data will overwrite the previous contents without confirmation from the user.

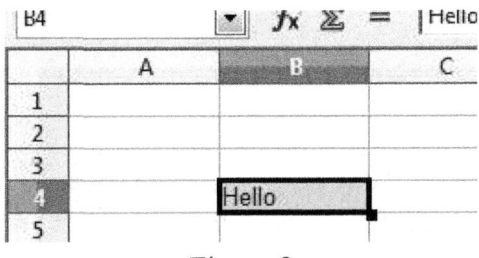

Figure 3

Note – If desired, the user can move a cell's data to a new location and also keep the data in its original location, by holding down the **CTRL** key before letting go of the left mouse button.

When working in OpenOffice Calc, it is possible to accidently drag and drop data to a new cell within the spreadsheet. If this happens and the user wishes to undo the unintentional drag and drop, they can use Calc's **Undo** feature. The Undo feature sets the spreadsheet back to its original form prior to the unwanted activity. This feature can be utilized by clicking the **Undo** button, located on the Toolbar; or by using the keyboard shortcut **CTRL + Z**.

Note – The Undo button looks like a curved arrow pointing to the left.

Figure 4

Growth & Assessment

1. What is the keyboard shortcut to undo an unintentional edit in Calc?

2. The drag and drop method is one way to move the data from one cell to another in OpenOffice Calc.

    a. TRUE

    b. FALSE

3. How would users move the contents of a cell to a new location without moving the original data?

Section 1.7 – Using Copy and Cut

Section Objective:

- Learn how to move data in a spreadsheet using copy and cut.

Moving Data Using Copy and Cut Techniques

When moving data in a spreadsheet, OpenOffice Calc offers alternatives to the drag and drop method. Calc allows users to move data from one cell to another, by using the Cut and Copy techniques. The Cut technique moves the data from one cell to a different cell, while deleting the data from the original cell. This technique is helpful when moving misplaced data in a spreadsheet. The Copy technique moves the data from one cell to a different cell, while keeping the data in the original cell as well. This technique is helpful when duplicating formulas, values, and labels keeps the user from having to reenter the data.

This section will cover how both of these techniques can be done. The first set of steps will explain how to use the Cut technique and the second set of steps will explain the Copy technique.

Using the Cut Technique

Step 1: Create a new Calc spreadsheet and enter text into one cell. After entering the text, select the cell.

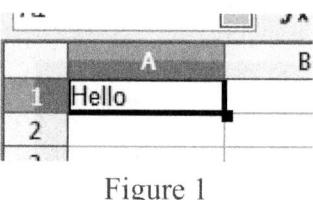

Figure 1

Step 2: Click **Edit**, located on the Menu Bar.

Step 3: From the Edit drop-down menu, click **Cut**. This will remove the text from the original cell.

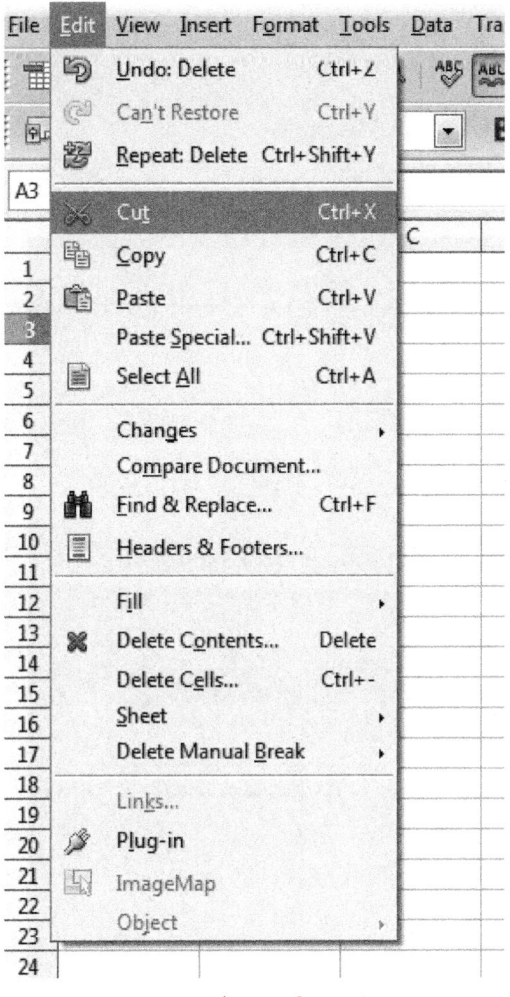

Figure 2

Note – The keyboard shortcut **CTRL + X** will also *Cut* the text from the original cell.

Step 4: Select a different cell.

Step 5: Once again, click **Edit**, located on the Menu Bar.

Step 6: From the Edit drop-down menu, select **Paste**. The text will then be inserted into the new cell.

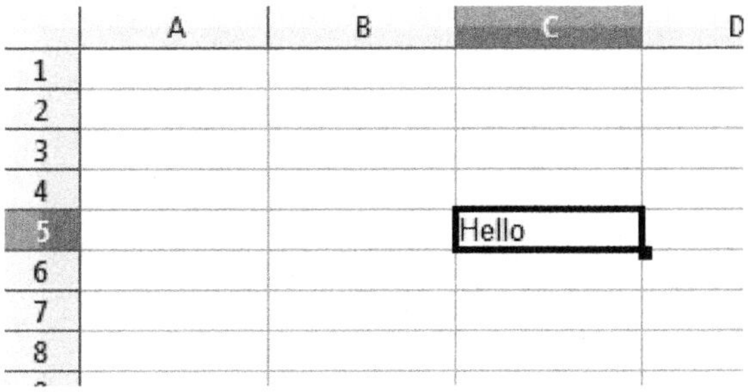

Figure 3

23

Note – The keyboard shortcut **CTRL + V** will also *Paste* the text into the new cell.

Using the Copy Technique

Step 1: In the Calc spreadsheet, enter text into a cell. After entering the text, select the cell.

Step 2: Click **Edit**, located on the Menu Bar.

Step 3: From the Edit drop-down menu, click **Copy**. This will copy the text and leave it unaltered in its original cell.

> **Note** – The keyboard shortcut **CTRL + C** will also *Copy* the text and leave it unaltered in its original cell.

Step 4: Select a different cell.

Step 5: Once again, click **Edit**, located on the Menu Bar.

Step 6: From the Edit drop-down menu, select **Paste**. The text will then be inserted into the new cell while remaining in the original cell as well.

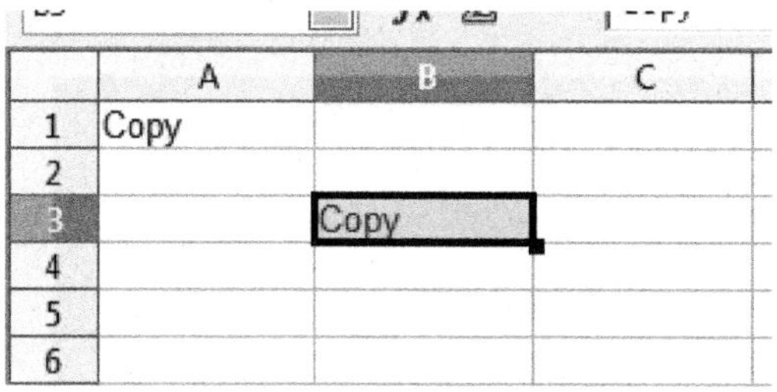

Figure 4

As mentioned above, the keyboard shortcut **CTRL + V** will also *Paste* the text into the new cell.

Growth & Assessment

1. What does the Cut feature do?

2. What is keyboard shortcut to *Cut* text?

3. The keyboard shortcut CTRL + C will *Copy* text.

    a. TRUE

    b. FALSE

4. What is an alternative to the Cut and Copy techniques?

Section 1.8 – Adding and Removing Columns and Rows

Section Objective:

- Learn how to add, and remove, columns and rows.

Adding Columns and Rows

OpenOffice Calc allows users to add columns and rows individually or in groups. This is helpful when a large amount of data needs to be inserted into a spreadsheet because it allows the user to easily add the required cells without having to add the individual rows and/or columns separately. The following steps explain how to add columns and rows in groups, as well as individually.

Adding Rows or Columns Individually

Step 1: Select a cell where an added column or row is wanted.

Step 2: Click **Insert**, located on the Menu Bar.

Step 3: From the Insert drop-down menu, select **Rows** or **Columns** (**Rows** will insert a row, **Columns** will insert a column).

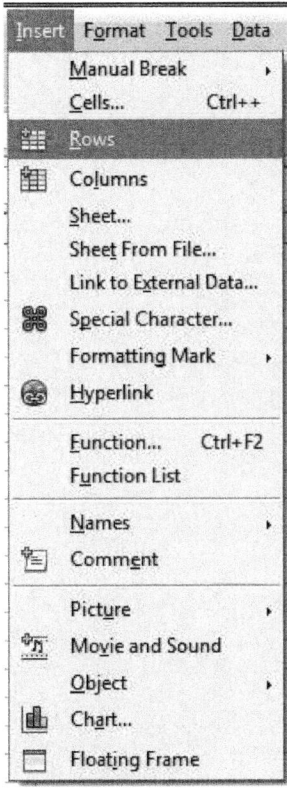

Figure 1

25

Note – Rows will always be inserted *above* the row in which the selected cell is located. **Columns** will always be inserted to the *left* of the column in which the selected cell is located.

Adding Rows or Columns in Groups

Step 1: Select the number of rows or columns needed by holding down the left mouse button on the first column or row, and dragging the cursor over the desired number of rows or columns until the needed amount is selected.

Step 2: Click **Insert**, located on the Menu Bar.

Step 3: From the Insert drop-down menu, select **Rows** or **Columns** depending on the type of selection made in **Step 1**.

Step 4: Once the desired option has been selected (Rows or Columns), the highlighted number identified in **Step 1** will be added to the spreadsheet.

Deleting Columns and Rows

OpenOffice Calc also allows users to delete unwanted rows and columns within a spreadsheet. This is helpful when working with data and trying to make predictions because once unneeded data and/or outliers are identified, the user can delete them to generate more accurate predictions.

Aside from adding columns and rows, Calc allows users to delete columns and rows individually or in groups. The steps below explain how both of these tasks are done.

Deleting Rows or Columns Individually

Step 1: Select a cell in the column or row that will be deleted.

Step 2: Right-click anywhere inside the cell. A quick menu will appear.

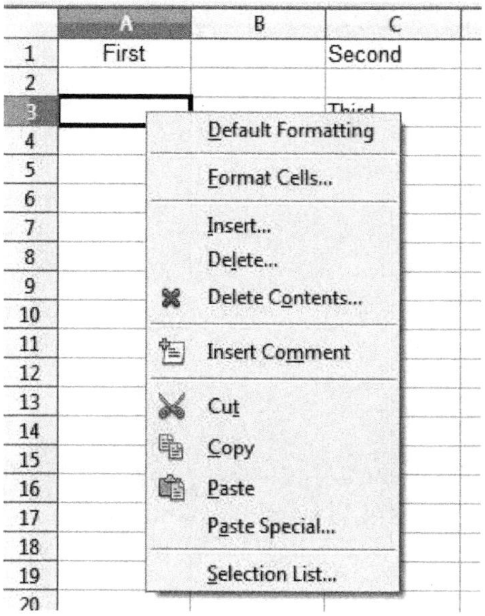

Figure 2

26

Step 3: From the quick menu, select **Delete**. The **Delete Cells** dialog box will appear.

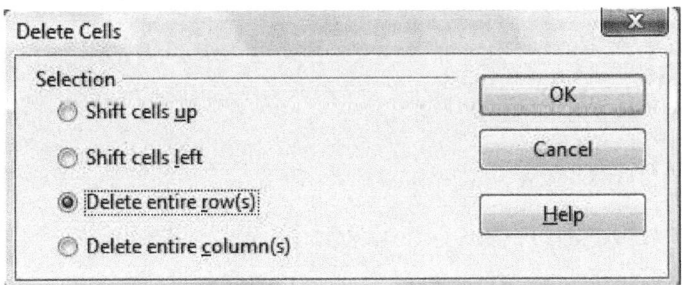

Figure 3

Step 4: Select the **Shift cells up** or **Shift cells left** to delete the cell.

Deleting Rows or Columns in Groups

Step 1: Select the number of rows or columns needed by holding down the left mouse button on the first column or row, and dragging the cursor over the desired number of rows or columns until the needed amount is selected.

Step 2: Right-click anywhere inside the selected cells. A quick menu will appear.

Step 3: From the quick menu, select **Delete**. The **Delete Cells** dialog box will appear.

Step 4: Select **Delete entire column(s)** or **Delete entire row(s)**, depending on the desired action, and click **OK**. The selected number of rows or columns will be deleted.

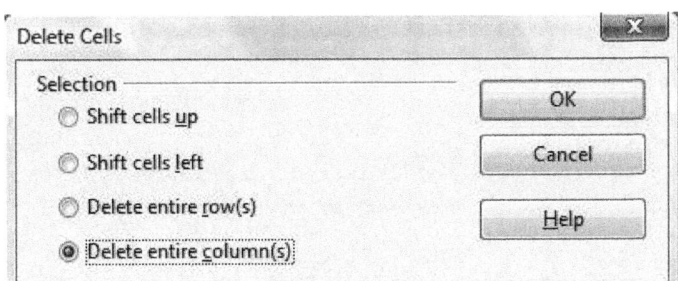

Figure 4

Growth & Assessment

1. Rows and columns can be deleted individually or in groups.

    a. TRUE

    b. FALSE

2. When would a user want to add rows and columns in groups?

3. When adding rows, where is the new row inserted?

4. When adding columns, where is the new column inserted?

27

Section 1.9 – Hiding and Revealing Columns and Rows

Section Objective:

- Learn how to hide and reveal columns and rows.

Hiding and Revealing Columns and Rows

OpenOffice Calc allows the user to hide columns and rows in the spreadsheet depending on the user's preference. At times, when working with data, certain columns and/or rows need to be displayed without the distractions of the other information stored in the spreadsheet. For example, a team of scientists are studying the growth of a particular plant species for an entire year. They use a spreadsheet to record data. Each day, the scientists record all of the environmental factors of the day such as, humidity, sunlight, rainfall, etc. After a year, the data has filled up the spreadsheet; there are hundreds of inter-connected rows and columns. The display of information is a clutter of numbers, comments, and observations. However, by hiding particular rows and columns, the scientists are able to target specific areas of interest. For instance, the scientists could isolate only the recorded daily rainfall during March.

This section will explain how to hide and reveal certain portions of the Calc spreadsheet without deleting needed information. The following steps outline how this is done.

Hiding Columns and Rows

Step 1: Create a new spreadsheet in Calc and enter text into a cell.

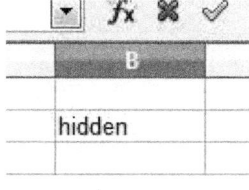

Figure 1

28

Step 2: Click on the cells **Column Heading** (A, B, C …), located at the top of the spreadsheet. This will select the entire column.

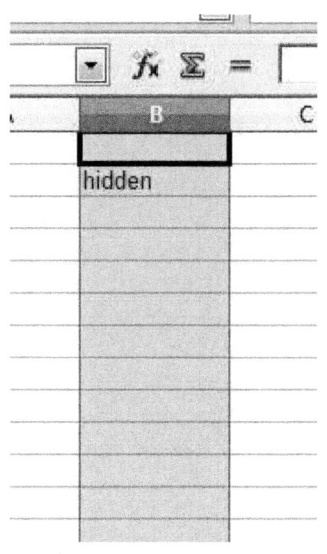

Figure 2

Step 3: Right-click the column heading. The **Quick Menu** will appear.

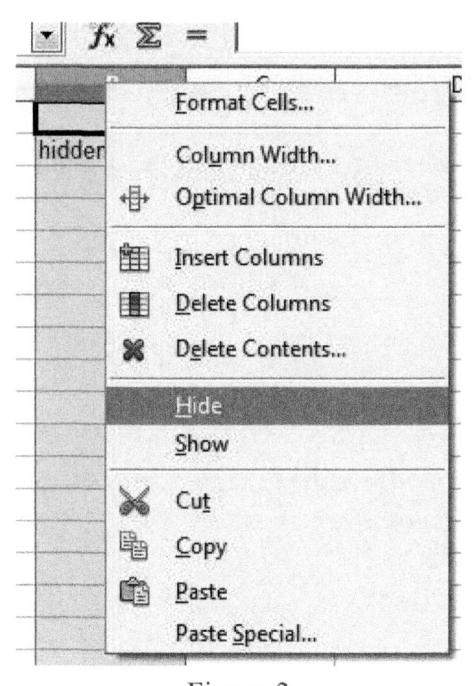

Figure 3

Step 4: Select **Hide** in the Quick Menu. This will cause the column to be **hidden**, meaning that the column's information is still saved in the cells, however it is not displayed.

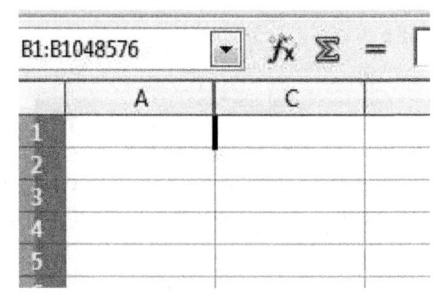

Figure 4

Note – A Row can be hidden the same way as a Column; however, instead of clicking on the Column heading (which is a letter), click on the Row heading (which is a number).

Revealing Columns and Rows

In OpenOffice Calc, revealing and hiding columns and rows is done the same way, with the exception being the selection made in the Quick Start menu. Since the steps above explained how to hide a column, the steps below will explain how to reveal a row.

Note – The following steps explain how a row is revealed after previously being hidden.

Step 1: Create a new spreadsheet in Calc and enter text into a cell.

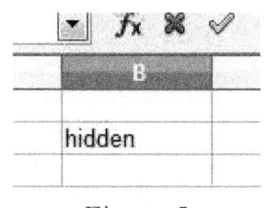

Figure 5

Step 2: Click on the cell's **Row Heading** (1, 2, 3 …), located on the left of the spreadsheet. This will select the entire row.

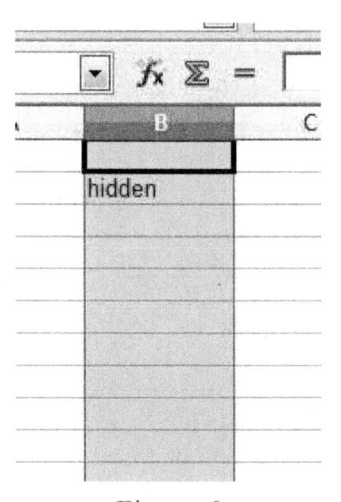

Figure 6

Step 3: Right-click the row heading. The **Quick Menu** will appear.

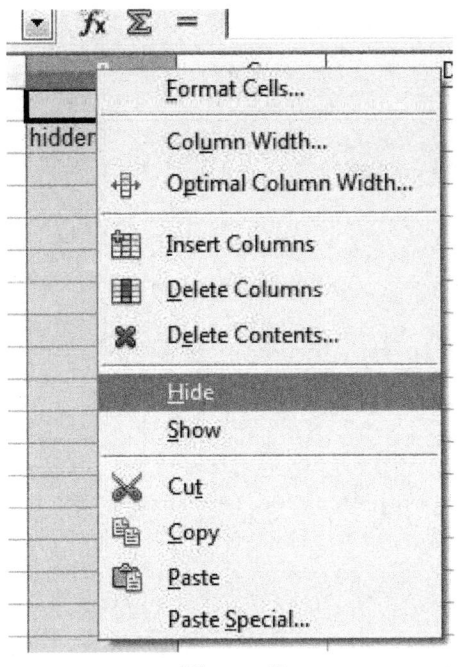

Figure 7

Step 4: Select **Show** in the Quick Menu. This will cause the row to be **revealed**, meaning that the row's information, which was previously hidden, is now displayed in the spreadsheet.

Growth & Assessment

1. Columns use numbers for headings.

    a. TRUE

    b. FALSE

2. Columns are the horizontal groups of cells.

    a. TRUE

    b. FALSE

3. Why would a user want to hide a row or column?

4. What do rows use for headings?

Section 1.10 – Hiding Cell Contents

Section Objective:

- Learn how to hide cell contents.

Hiding Cell Contents

OpenOffice Calc allows users to hide the contents within a cell. This is a useful feature if the cell contents do not need to be viewed or printed. The steps to hide the contents within a cell are outlined below.

Step 1: Create a new Calc spreadsheet and enter text into a cell. Make sure that the cell is still selected after entering the data.

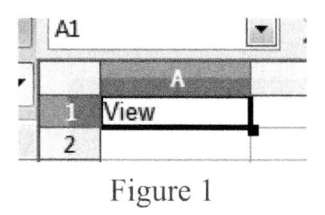

Figure 1

Step 2: Click **Format**, located on the Menu Bar.

Step 3: From in the Format drop-down menu, click **Cells…**. The **Format Cells** dialog box will appear.

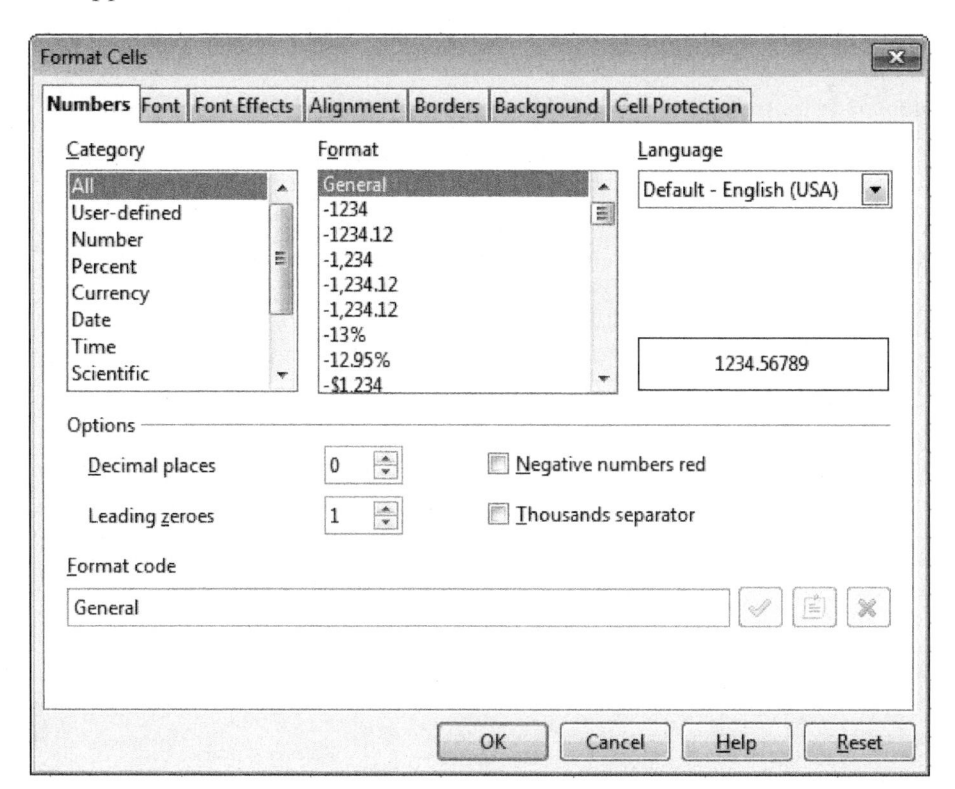

Figure 2

Step 4: Within the **Format Cells** dialog box, select the **Numbers** tab.

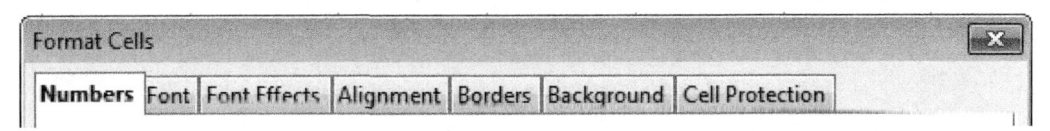

Figure 3

Step 5: Under **Category**, select **User-defined**.

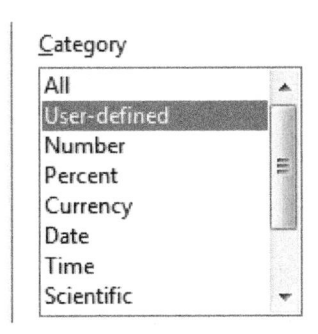

Figure 4

Step 6: Under **Format code**, type ";;;" into the textbox.

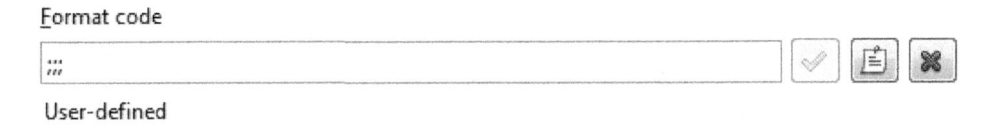

Figure 5

Step 7: Click **OK**. The selected cells will be hidden.

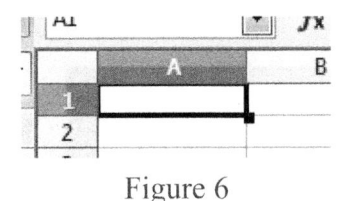

Figure 6

Revealing the Cell Contents

Writer allows users to reveal, or redisplay, the cell contents after it has been hidden. This is helpful when the user needs to edit the hidden cells or needs to reference the information within the cells. The following steps explain how this is done.

Step 1: Select the cell that was previously hidden.

Step 2: Click **Format**, located on the Menu Bar.

Step 3: From in the Format drop-down menu, click **Cells…**. The **Format Cells** dialog box will appear.

Step 4: Within the **Format Cells** dialog box, select the **Numbers** tab.

Step 5: Under **Category**, select **All**.

Step 6: Under **Format code**, select **General**. The dialog box will refresh to display options corresponding to the selected category.

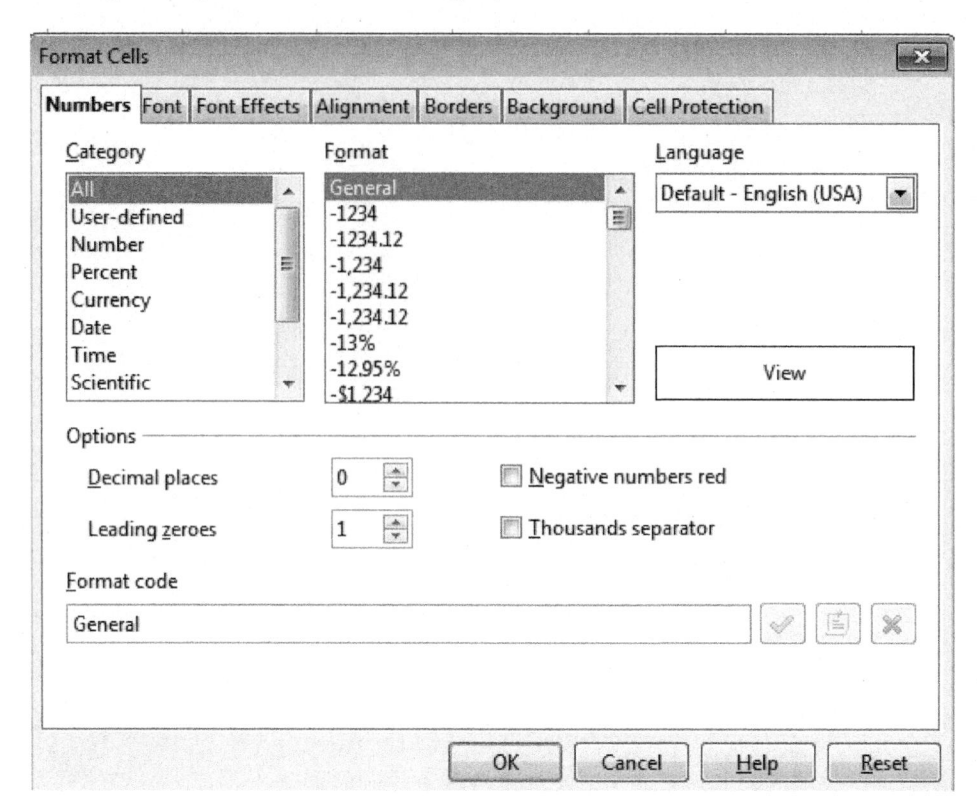

Figure 7

Step 7: Click **OK**. The cells will reappear.

Growth & Assessment

1. OpenOffice Calc allows users to hide the contents within a cell.

    a. TRUE

    b. FALSE

2. Under which section will a user select **User-defined** when following the steps to hide cell contents?

3. What is the Format code to hide cell contents?

4. Once a cell's contents are hidden, they are hidden permanently.

    a. TRUE

    b. FALSE

Section 1.11 – Freezing and Unfreezing Panes

Section Objective:

- Learn how to Freeze and Unfreeze Panes.

Freezing and Unfreezing Panes

The Freeze Panes feature in OpenOffice Calc allows users to view different sections of a spreadsheet at the same time. A user is able to make specific rows and/or columns visible while scrolling within the spreadsheet. This feature is very important when the data from one section needs to be referenced or moved to another section within the same spreadsheet. The following steps outline how to use the Freeze Panes feature, and will explain how to unfreeze portions of the spreadsheet as well.

Freezing Panes

To freeze panes (certain areas within a spreadsheet), the user needs to select the cells that will be frozen together. This can be done by clicking the cell below and to the right of the last cell in the range that will be frozen. The selected cell (identified in **Step 1**) will function as an indicator. All cells above and to the left of the selected cell will be frozen. The selected cell will not be included in the range.

Step 1: Create a new Calc spreadsheet and select a cell.

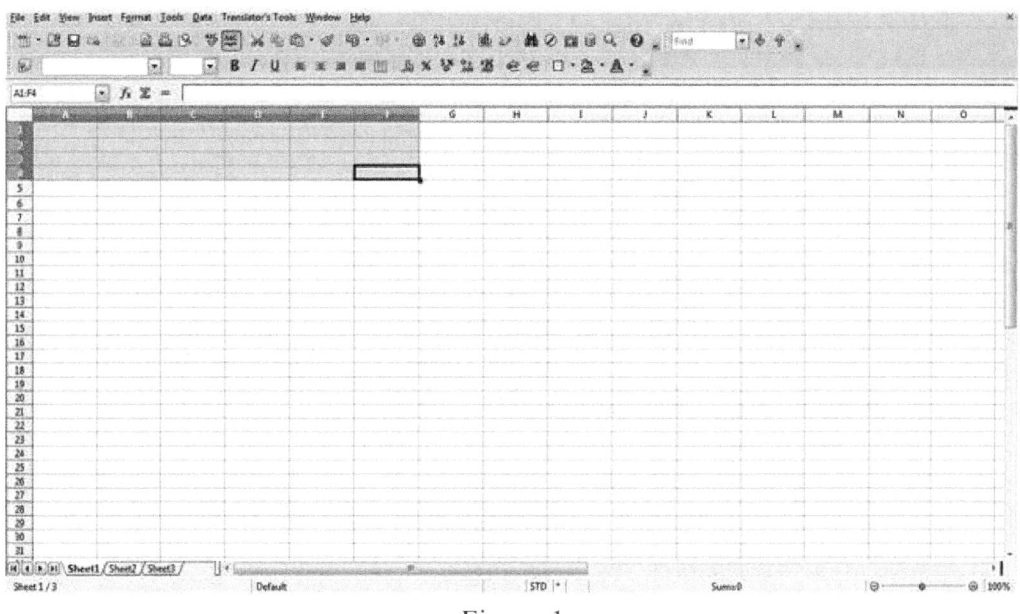

Figure 1

Step 2: Click **Window**, located on the Menu Bar.

35

Step 3: From in the **Window** menu, click **Freeze**. All of the cells above and to the left of the selected cell, or indicator, will be frozen.

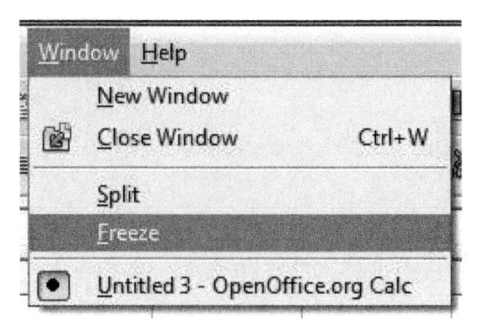

Figure 2

If the user scrolls through the spreadsheet, the previously frozen pane of selected cells will remain in place as the user moves down the spreadsheet.

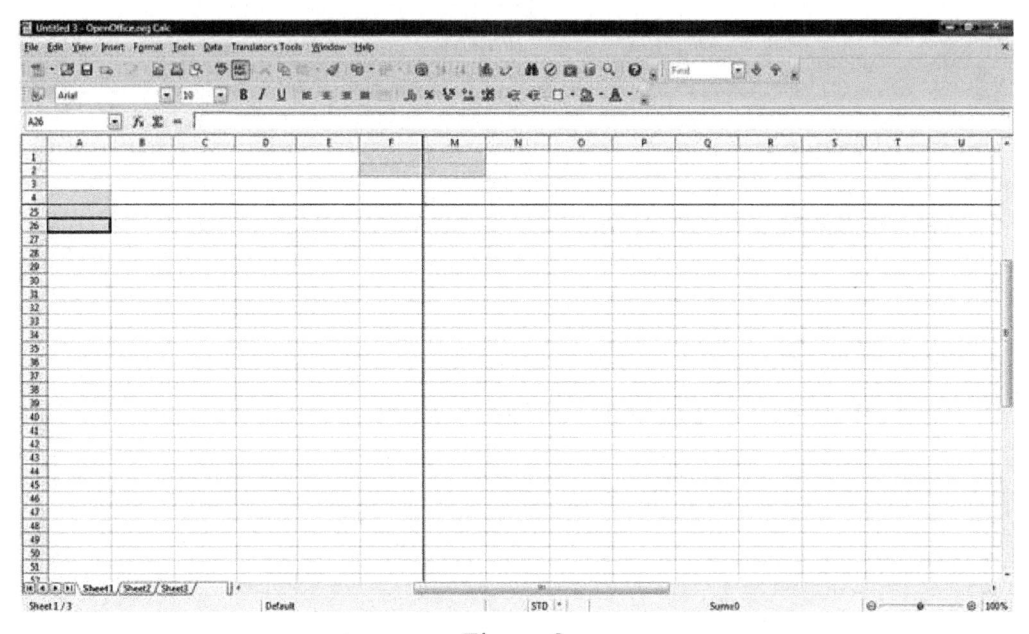

Figure 3

Unfreeze Panes

If the user would like to **Unfreeze** the panes that were previously frozen, follow the steps below.

Step 1: Click **Window**, located on the Menu Bar.

Step 2: From in the Window drop-down menu, click **Freeze**. Once clicked, the checkmark next to **Freeze** will be removed, indicating that all panes are unfrozen.

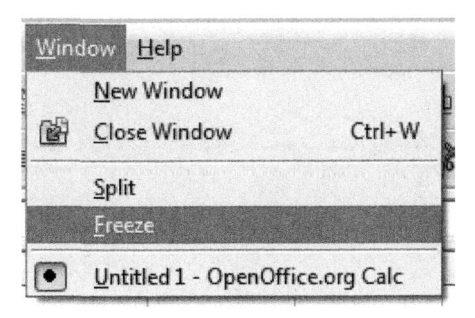

Figure 4

Growth & Assessment

1. Why is the Freeze feature in Calc important?

2. When a cell is chosen and **Freeze** is selected, which cells are frozen?

3. Selecting **Freeze** a second time will unfreeze the cells.

    a. TRUE

    b. FALSE

Section 1.12 – Using Split Screen and the Multiple Page Feature

Section Objectives:

- Learn how to use split screen.

- Learn how to view multiple copies of the same spreadsheet.

The Split Screen and Multiple Page Features

OpenOffice Calc has two features that allow a user to view different sections of a spreadsheet at the same time. The **Split Screen** and **Multiple Page** features are useful when referencing different sections of a larger spreadsheet in Calc. The steps below will outline how to use both of these features.

Using Split Screen

Step 1: Create a new spreadsheet in Calc and select a cell. Similar to other features in Calc, the cell selected is used as the identifier, meaning that all cells above and to the left of the selected cell will be split.

Step 2: Click **Window**, located on the Menu Bar.

Step 3: From the Window drop-down menu, click **Split**. The spreadsheet will split into four sections.

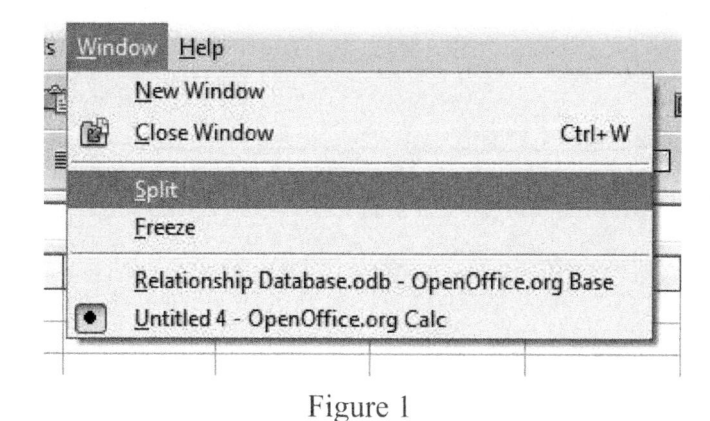

Figure 1

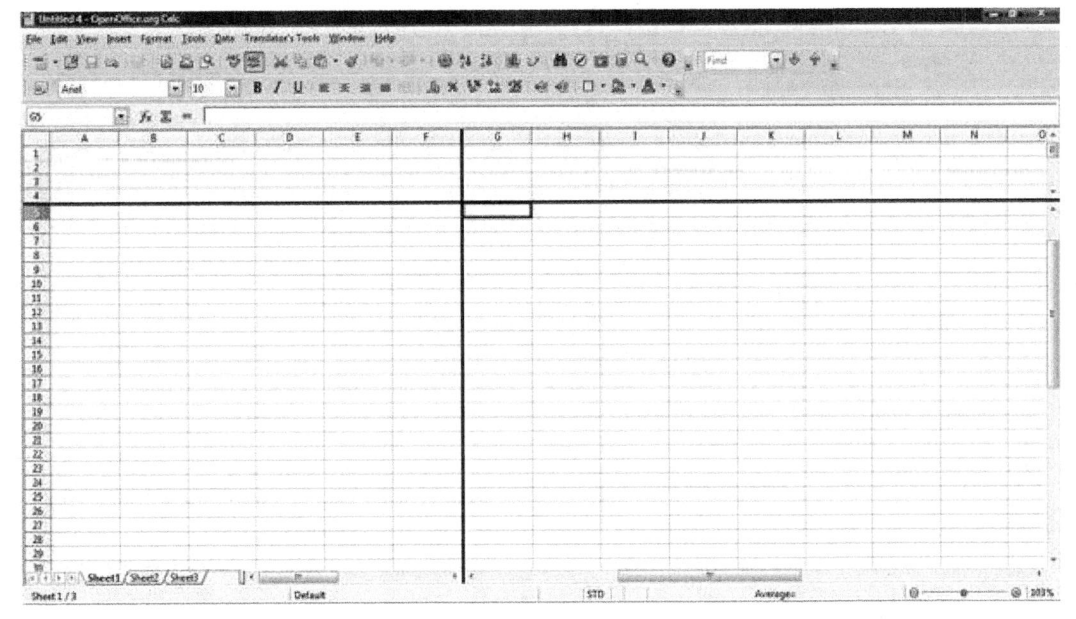

Figure 2

Note – Click **Split** a second time to merge the four split sections.

Using the Multiple Page Feature

Calc allows users to view multiple copies of the spreadsheet by using the **Multiple Page** feature. The following steps explain how this is done.

Step 1: Click **Window**, located on the Menu Bar.

Step 2: From the Window drop-down menu, click **New Window**. By repeating this step, the user creates multiple copies of the spreadsheet.

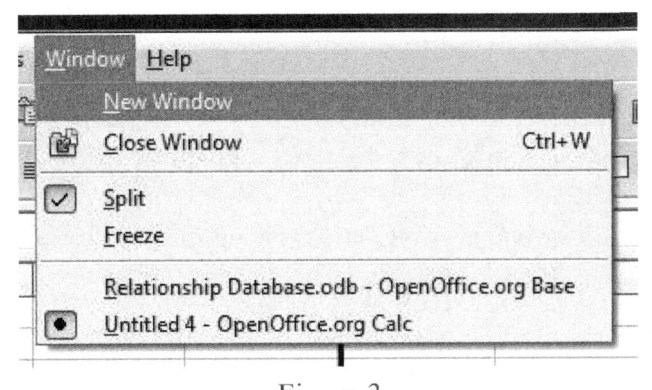

Figure 3

For each new spreadsheet created, there will be a new tab opened on the desktop application bar. The name of the document will be displayed with a number beside it. The number identifies which version of the document it is.

Figure 4

39

Note – Any changes made to one version, will show up in all versions of the document.

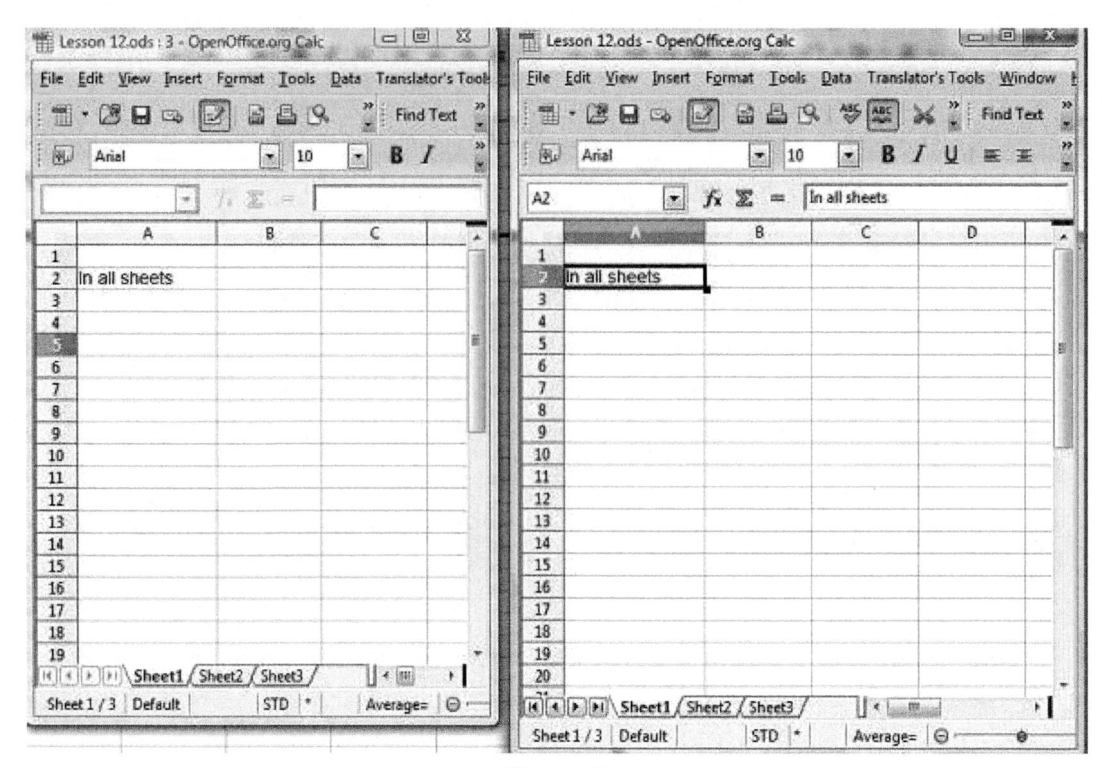

Figure 5

Growth & Assessment

1. Split allows users to split a spreadsheet into four parts.

    a. TRUE

    b. FALSE

2. When a cell is chosen and **Split** is selected, which cells are frozen?

3. Any changes made to one version, will show up in all versions of the document.

    a. TRUE

    b. FALSE

4. What does **New Window** do within the **Multiple Page** feature?

Section 1.13 – Using the Merge and Center Button

Section Objective:

- Learn how to use the Merge and Center button.

Using the Merge and Center Buttons

OpenOffice Calc allows users to easily create titles in a spreadsheet by providing two essential features: **Merge** and **Center**. The **Merge Cells** feature in Calc will combine multiple cells into one single cell. The **Center** feature will center the text within the middle of the merged cells. Together, these two buttons allow the user to create a title, header, or any other needed identification within a spreadsheet.

Using the Merge Button

Step 1: Create a new document in Calc and select a cell within the first spreadsheet.

Step 2: Using the left mouse button, drag the cursor from the selected cell over the desired number of cells. This will highlight which cells will be merged.

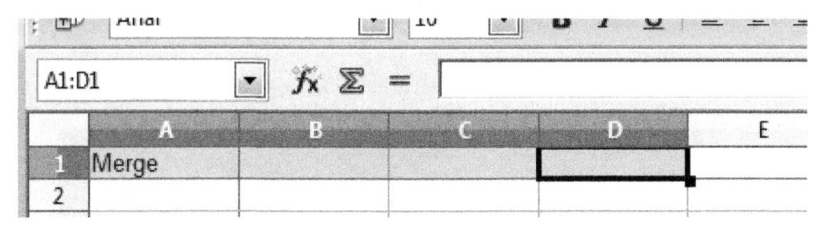

Figure 1

Step 3: Click **Format**, located on the Menu Bar.

Step 4: From the Format drop-down menu, select **Merge Cells**. The highlighted cells will merge into a single cell.

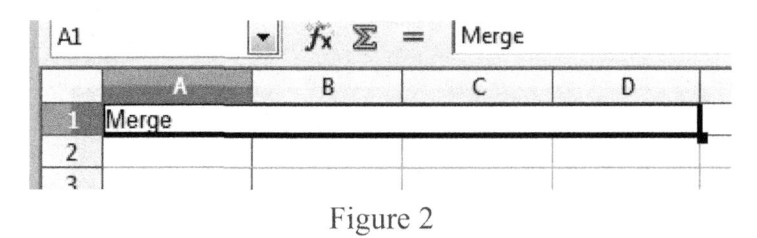

Figure 2

Note – After a cell merge, if two or more selected cells have data within them, Calc will display the information from the cell closest to the top left corner of the spreadsheet and will delete all other data.

Step 5: If the needed data is not already contained within the merged cell, enter the data. Once the data has been entered into the cell, select the cell and click the **Align Center Horizontally** button, located on the Toolbar. This will center the text within the merged cell.

Figure 3

Note – Pressing **CTRL + E** will also center the data within a merged cell.

Note – The **Merge Cells** button, located on the toolbar, will also merge highlighted cells.

Writer allows the user to undo an unwanted cell merge. This is helpful when a user needs to reorganize a spreadsheet and add or delete titles and headers. The following steps explain how this is done.

Step 1: Select the cell that was previously merged.

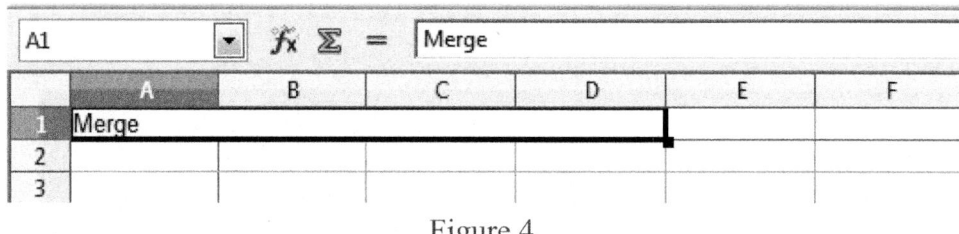

Figure 4

Step 2: Click **Format**, located on the Menu Bar.

Step 3: From the Format drop-down menu, select **Merge Cells** a second time. The application will automatically insert the cells, and all data within the cells, back to their original form.

Note – The **Merge Cells** button, located on the toolbar, will also undo a previously merged cell. This is done by selecting the single cell and clicking the **Merge Cells** button. Once clicked, the merged cell will split back into its individual cells.

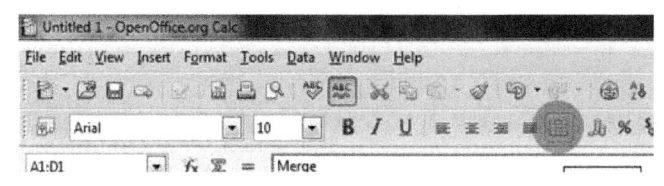

Figure 5

Growth & Assessment

1. What two features in Calc allow users to easily create headers?

2. What is the keyboard shortcut used to center data within a merged cell?

3. Clicking the **Merge Cells** button a second time will undo the merge.

    a. TRUE

    b. FALSE

4. What button, located on the Toolbar, will center the data within a cell?

Section 1.14 – Adding ClipArt to a Spreadsheet

Section Objective:

- Learn how to add ClipArt to a spreadsheet.

Adding ClipArt to a Spreadsheet

Spreadsheets created in OpenOffice Calc will usually be used for collecting data; however, there may be times when a user wants to add a visual appeal. Calc uses ClipArt to accomplish this. ClipArt are digital images (mostly cartoonish). Inserting ClipArt into a spreadsheet is an easy way to add creativity and design elements. ClipArt can be added to spreadsheets for presentations as a way to draw attention to the data, or ClipArt can be added to broachers, menus, or other documents that require a visual appeal.

Before a user adds ClipArt to a spreadsheet, additional ClipArt must be added to the Calc application. This can be done by following the steps below.

Importing ClipArt

Step 1: Go to the following link: *http://extensions.services.openoffice.org/en/project/oxygenoffice-gallery*. This will access the OpenOffice ClipArt extension page.

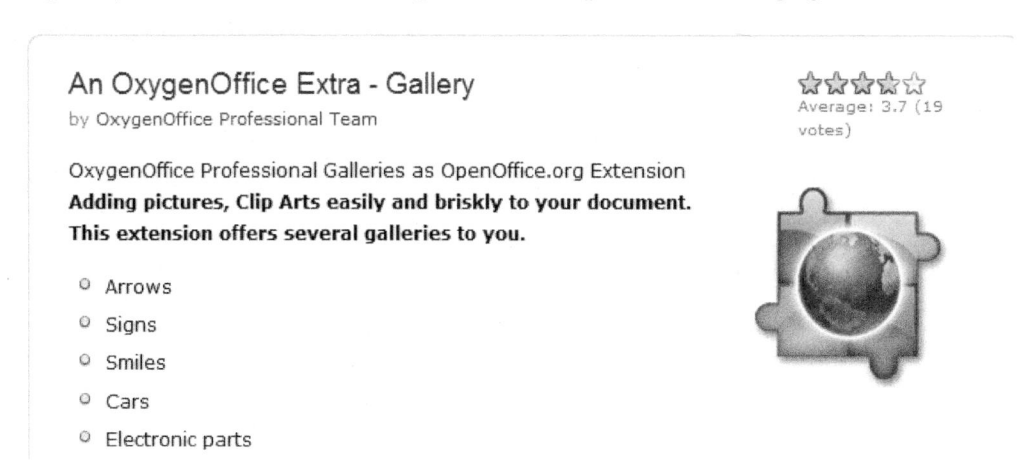

Figure 1

Step 2: Scroll through the various pages of ClipArt and select a style by clicking the ClipArt icon.

Step 3: Click the **Get It!** button to be directed to the **Download** page.

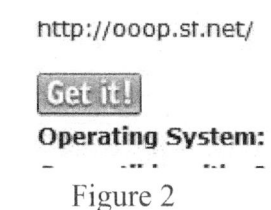

Figure 2

Step 4: Click on the **manual download link** to begin the download.

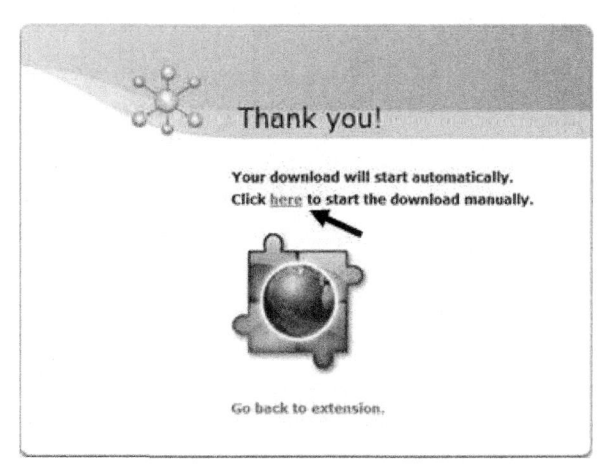

Figure 3

Note – If using Google Chrome, the File Download prompt will appear in the lower-left corner of the window. Once selected, the user will be taken to Step 5.

Step 5: When prompted, click **Open** on the File **Download** window.

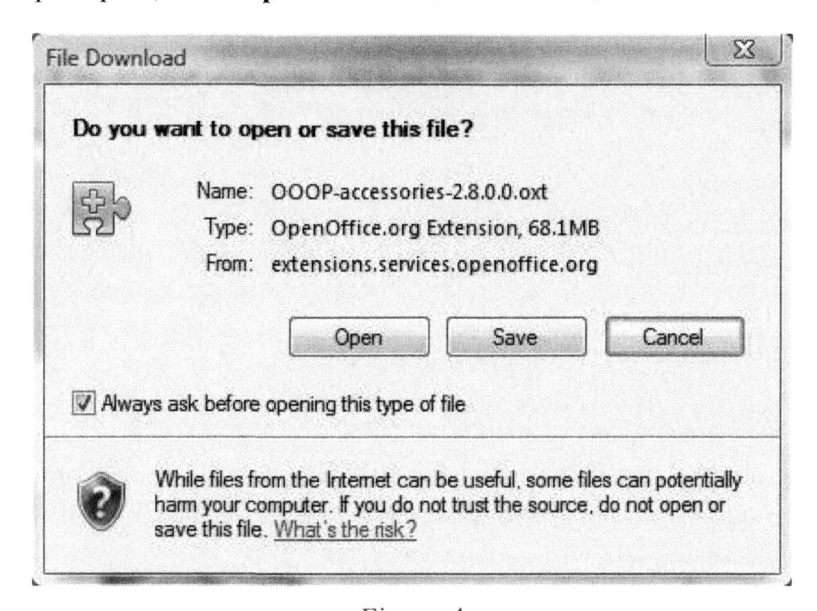

Figure 4

Step 5: The next prompt will confirm with the user that ClipArt is to be installed. Click **OK**, and then click **Accept** to accept the license agreement.

45

Figure 5

Step 6: The Extension Manager window will show that the chosen ClipArt has been added to Calc. Click **Close**, and the new graphics are available to use within the Calc application.

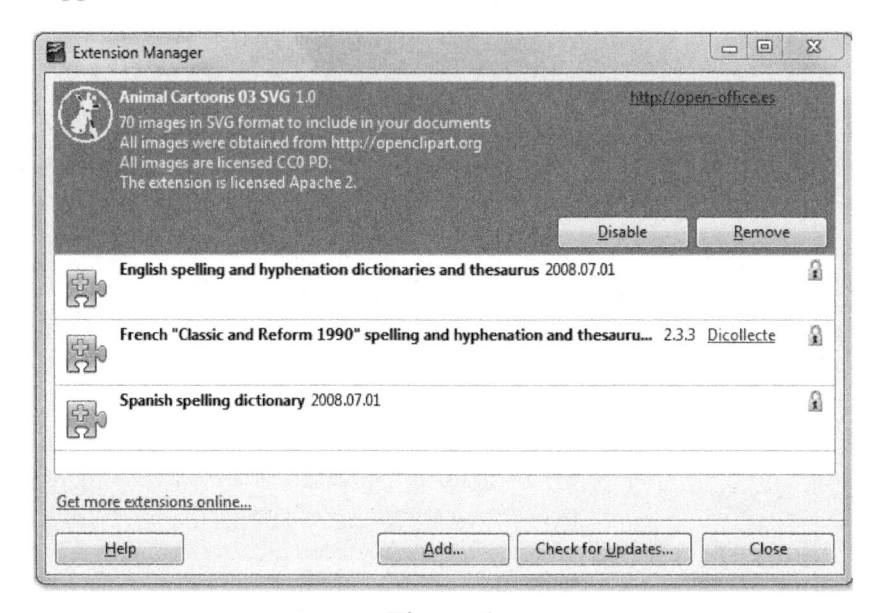

Figure 6

Inserting ClipArt

Once the collection of ClipArt has been added to Calc, the user has the ability to insert art by browsing through the **Gallery**, and selecting the preferred artwork. The following steps outline how this is done.

Step 1: Click **Tools**, located on the Menu Bar.

Step 2: From the Tools drop-down menu, select **Gallery**. The ClipArt task pane will appear at the top of the page window.

Figure 7

Step 3: Along the left-hand side of the task pane, there will be different folders displaying the types of ClipArt available. Select the preferred ClipArt type.

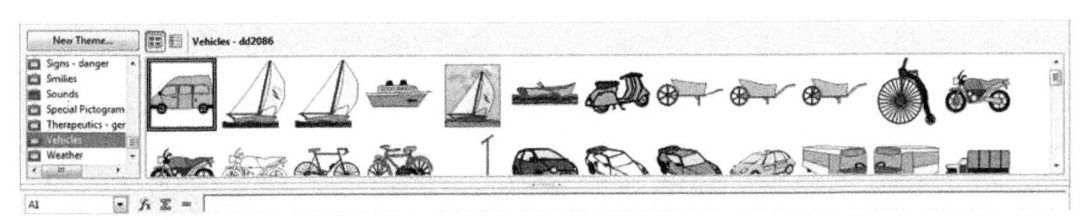

Figure 8

Step 4: View the various pieces of ClipArt presented in the task pane. When the preferred image is found, click and hold the image with left mouse button, and drag it into the spreadsheet.

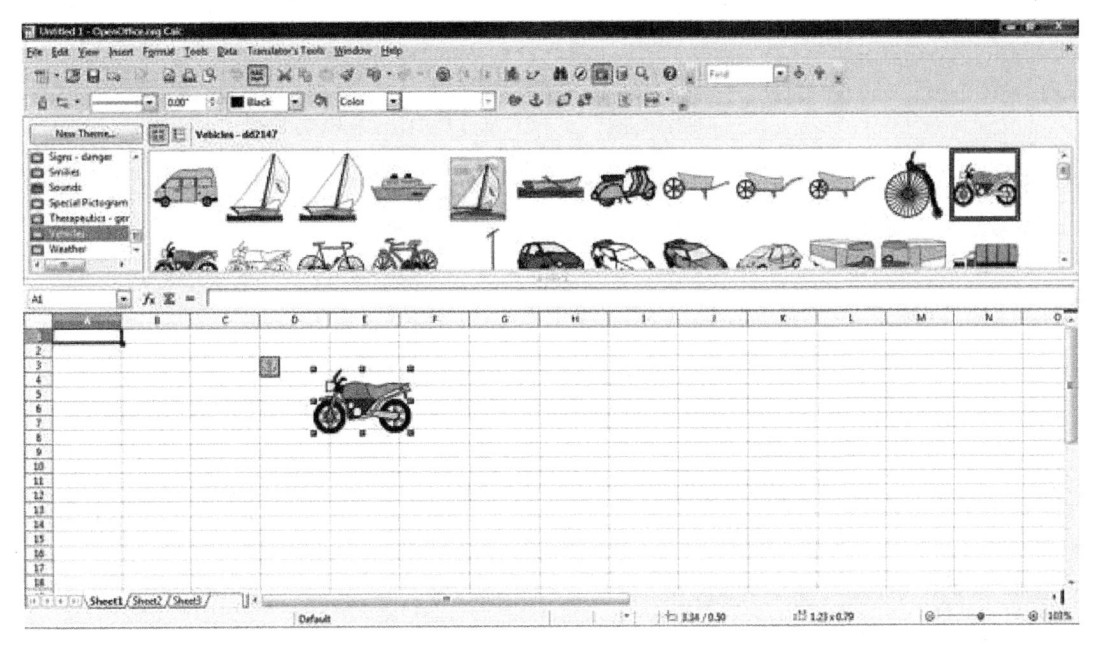

Figure 9

Growth & Assessment

1. Utilizing **ClipArt** is an easy way to add creativity and design elements to a spreadsheet.

    a. TRUE

    b. FALSE

2. Where is **ClipArt** located in Calc?

3. What is **ClipArt**?

Section 1.15 – Searching for Data in a Spreadsheet

Section Objective:

- Learn how to search for data in a spreadsheet.

Searching for Data in a Spreadsheet

When working with data, being able to find specific information is important. OpenOffice Calc allows users to easily find data within a spreadsheet by using the **Find & Replace** feature. The following steps explain how this feature is used to find specific information stored within the spreadsheet.

Step 1: Open a previously saved Calc spreadsheet.

Step 2: Click **Edit**, located on the Menu Bar.

Step 3: From the Edit drop-down menu, select **Find & Replace**. The **Find & Replace** dialog box will appear.

Note – The keyboard shortcut **CTRL + F** will also open the **Find & Replace** dialog box.

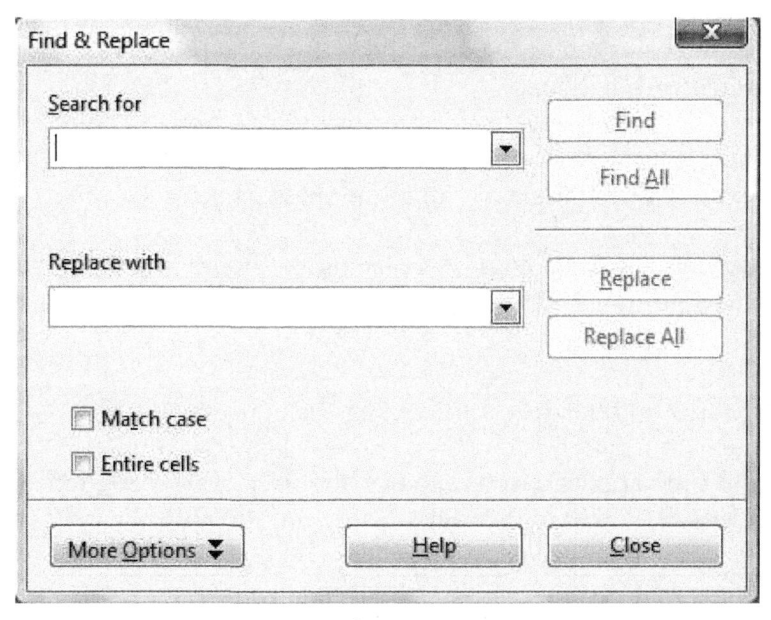

Figure 1

Step 4: In the **Search for** textbox, enter text that is somewhere within the spreadsheet and then click **Find**.

Step 5: Once Find has been clicked, the first occurrence of the text entered into the textbox will be highlighted within the spreadsheet.

Note – To find all of the occurrences of the text entered into the **Search for** textbox, continue clicking **Find** until the entire spreadsheet has been searched.

Step 6: Once the desired amount of occurrences have been found within the spreadsheet, click **Close**.

> **Note** – Rather than clicking through the entire spreadsheet to find every occurrence of the text, Calc allows the user to find every occurrence at once. This can be done by clicking the **Find All** button, located in the **Find & Replace** dialog box.

Replacing Data within a Spreadsheet

OpenOffice Calc allows the user to not only find specific text within a spreadsheet, but also replace the found text with different text. This can be done by using the same feature, the **Find & Replace** dialog box. The user has two options when using this feature; the user can replace all occurrences of found text, or can view each occurrence before deciding if replacing the text is necessary. The following steps explain how this is done.

Step 1: Open a previously saved Calc spreadsheet.

Step 2: Click **Edit**, located on the Menu Bar.

Step 3: From the Edit drop-down menu, select **Find & Replace**. The **Find & Replace** dialog box will appear.

Step 4: In the **Search for** textbox, enter the text that needs to be replaced.

Step 5: In the **Replace** portion of the dialog box, enter the preferred replacement text into the **Replace with** textbox.

Step 6: To find the first occurrence of the text entered in **Step 4**, click **Find**. The first occurrence of the text will be highlighted within the spreadsheet.

Step 7: Here, the user has the option of replacing the highlighted text with the preferred text entered in **Step 5**. To replace the text, click **Replace**. To leave the text in its original state, click **Find**.

Step 8: Repeat **Step 7** until all necessary text has been replaced.

Step 9: When the Calc application has shown the user every occurrence of the text entered in **Step 4**, a dialog box will appear with the message "OpenOffice Calc has searched to the end of the document. Do you want to continue at the beginning?" If the user would like to go back through the document, they can do so by clicking **OK**. If not, click **Close**.

> **Note** – As stated above, Calc allows the user to replace every occurrence of the text at once. This can be done by clicking the **Replace All** button, located in the **Find & Replace** dialog box.

Growth & Assessment

1. What feature in OpenOffice Calc allows users to easily find data within a spreadsheet?

2. What is the keyboard shortcut to open the **Find & Replace** dialog box?

3. Which button allows users to find every occurrence of a text?

4. A user can replace every occurrence of a text at once using the **Find All** button.

    a. TRUE

    b. FALSE

Unit Two

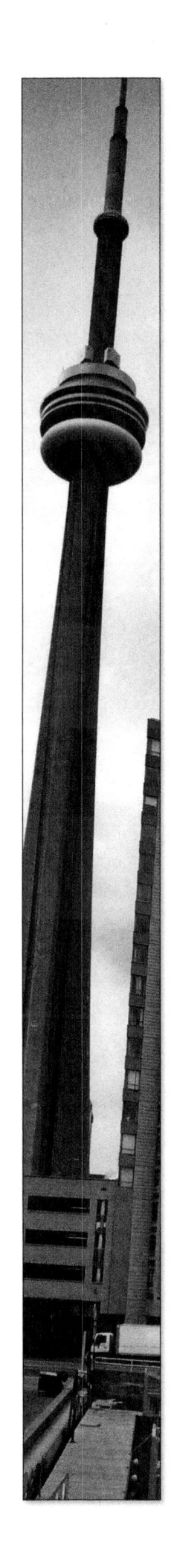

Section 2.1 – Calculating Data   54

Section 2.2 – Naming Groups of Data   56

Section 2.3 – Creating Formulas   60

Section 2.4 – Different Types of Operators   62

Section 2.5 – Using the Detective Tool   64

Section 2.6 – Spreadsheet Auditing   68

Section 2.7 – Adding Subtotals to a Spreadsheet   70

Section 2.8 – Adding a Chart to a Spreadsheet   74

Section 2.9 – Entering Data into Multiple Spreadsheets   80

Section 2.10 – Using Screen Filters to Limit Data   83

Section 2.11 – Creating a Custom Filter   86

Section 2.12 – Working With Advanced Filters   91

Section 2.13 – Getting Running Totals   96

Section 2.14 – Improving Accuracy of Spreadsheets   98

Section 2.15 – Sorting Data   101

Section 2.1 – Calculating Data

Section Objective:

- Learn why calculating data is important.

Why Calculate Data?

In OpenOffice Calc users have the ability to reduce pages of data into subtotals and averages. Performing these calculations help users make sense of the raw data in a spreadsheet. In order to perform the necessary calculations, the user must build a formula. In Calc, a formula is a series of mathematical instructions that a user enters into a cell in order to perform some type of calculation. Calc allows users to build formulas by hand, or by using the point-and-click method. Once the formula has been created, it helps the user convert the raw data into usable figures by performing the necessary calculations.

All formulas share the same basic characteristics. The following summarizes these similarities:

- Each formula is entered into a single cell.
- All formulas will begin with an Equal Sign [=].

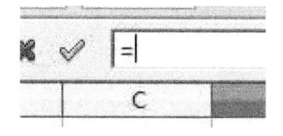

Figure 1

- Calc will calculate the result of a formula each time the data for the formula is updated.
- All formulas will return either a number (which is the most common) or a Boolean (True or False).
- Formulas can be viewed by selecting the cell and looking in the Formula Bar.

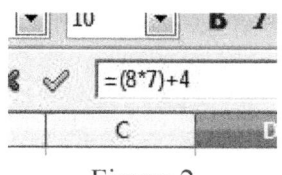

Figure 2

- Formulas can evaluate a combination of numbers the user inputs or the contents of other cells.

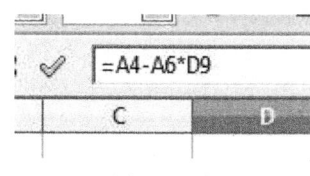

Figure 3

Growth & Assessment

1. In order to perform the necessary calculations, users must build a formula.

    a. TRUE

    b. FALSE

2. What do formulas do in Calc?

3. What do all formulas begin with?

4. Formulas can evaluate a combination of numbers the user inputs or the contents of other cells.

    a. TRUE

    b. FALSE

Section 2.2 – Naming Groups of Data

Section Objective:

- Learn about naming groups of data.

Naming Groups of Data

OpenOffice Calc allows users to assign descriptive names to cells and ranges. A **Range** refers to an adjacent group of cells within a spreadsheet. By naming ranges and other cells, users can better organize spreadsheets and refer back to specific data by searching for the range name.

Naming cells and ranges of data within Calc is helpful when creating formulas and mathematical equations. When inserting a formula into a cell, users can insert a range name into the formula rather than inserting all of the data contained within the range. Assigning these descriptive names to a group of data is done by going through the **Define Database Range** dialog box. The following steps outline how this is done.

Step 1: Open a previously saved Calc spreadsheet.

Step 2: Select the cells that will be included in the range. This is done by using the left mouse button to highlight the preferred group of cells.

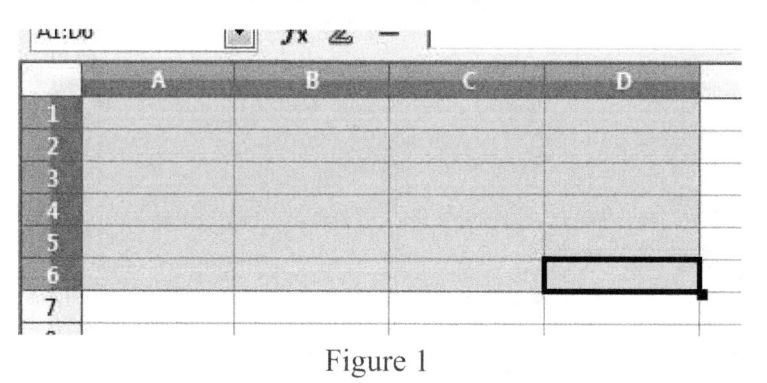

Figure 1

Step 3: Click **Data**, located on the Menu Bar.

Step 4: From the Data drop-down menu, select **Define Range**. The **Define Database Range** dialog box will appear.

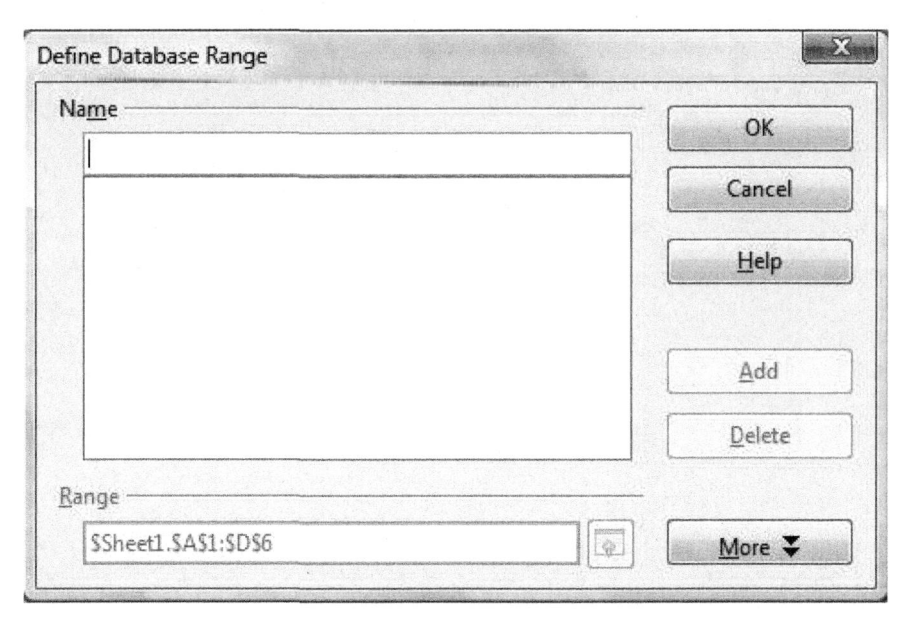

Figure 2

Note – When the **Define Database Range** dialog box is opened, the cells highlighted in **Step 2** will already be entered into the **Range** textbox.

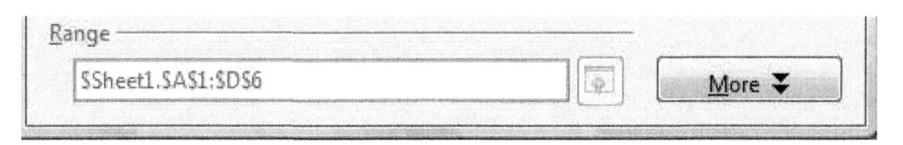

Figure 3

Step 5: In the **Name** textbox, enter a name for the range of cells.

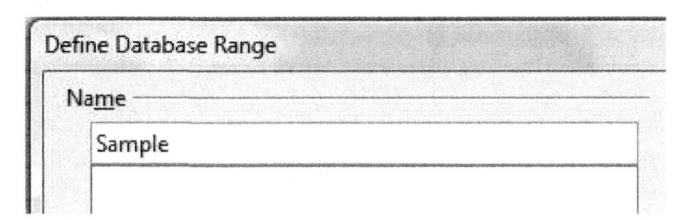

Figure 4

Step 6: Click **Add**. The new named range will be added to the box below.

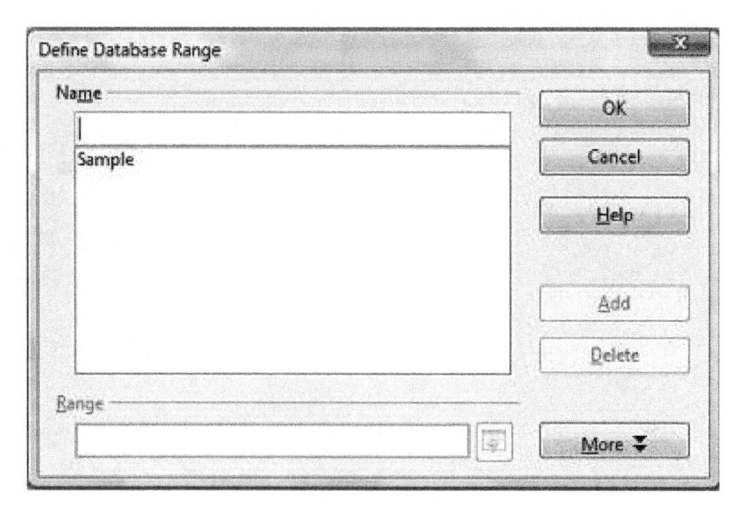

Figure 5

Step 7: Once the range name has been added, click **OK**. The Define Database Range dialog box will close.

Once the range name has been added, the user can access the range and apply it to formulas within the Calc application.

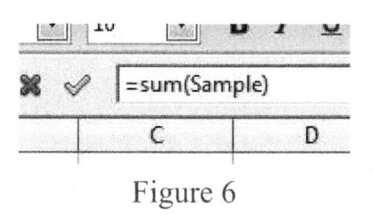

Figure 6

Using the Name Box

Calc also allows users to create a range of names by using the **Name Box**. The following steps explain how this is done.

Step 1: Select the cells that will be included in the range. As stated above, this is done by using the left mouse button to highlight the desired group of cells.

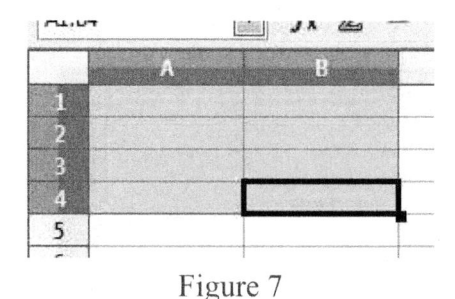

Figure 7

Step 2: In the **Name Box**, highlight the name that is displayed.

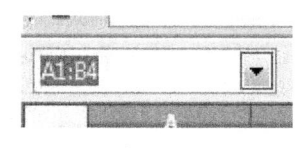

Figure 8

Step 3: Type the desired name for the range.

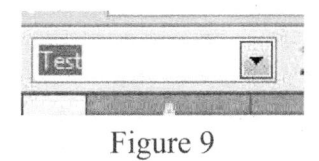

Figure 9

Step 4: Press **ENTER**. The selected cell range will now be referred to by the range name specified in **Step 3,** and can be used when creating formulas and equations.

Growth & Assessment

1. What Calc feature allows users to create a range of names?

2. What is a **Range**?

3. Naming cells and ranges of data within Calc is helpful when creating formulas and mathematical equations.

    a. TRUE

    b. FALSE

4. Where would users assign descriptive names to a group of data?

Section 2.3 – Creating Formulas

Section Objective:

- Learn how to create formulas to calculate data.

Creating Formulas in Calc

In Calc, a formula is a series of mathematical instructions that the user enters into a cell in order to perform some type of calculation. Calc allows users to build formulas by hand, or by using the point-and-click method. Once the formula has been created, it helps the user convert the raw data into usable figures by performing the necessary calculations. Formulas can also be used to link to other spreadsheets and spreadsheet files. This is helpful when a project requires a lot of data analysis and multiple spreadsheets are used.

Formulas, as described above, are an important aspect of OpenOffice Calc. It is important for users to understand how to write and enter formulas, in order to utilize this feature. When writing a formula, there are three elements which must be included for it to work properly:

- An equals sign [=] at the beginning of the formula.

- **Operands** – These are values or cell references that will be used to produce the result of the formula.

- **Operators** – These are the commands to add, subtract, or perform other actions with the operands.

To provide an example of **operands** and **operators**, a very basic formula would be written like this: **=A1-B1**

In this example, the cell references **A1** and **B1** are the **operands**, the **[-]** is the **operator**; the selected cell would contain the difference of the values in cells **A1** and **B1**.

Depending on what type of mathematical calculation is needed, formulas can be basic or complex; however, all formulas must be created using the same basic steps. Without these steps, even the simplest formula cannot be written. The basic steps needed to create a formula are outlined below.

Step 1: Select the preferred cell where the formula's results will be displayed.

Step 2: To begin the formula, enter the equal sign [=] into the formula bar.

Step 3: Click the first cell to be included into the formula, or type the cell reference name which would need to have been created previously.

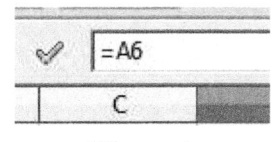

Figure 1

Step 4: Type the first **operand**.

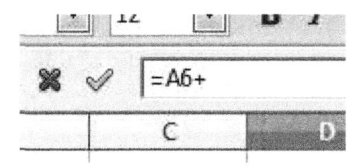

Figure 2

Step 5: Click or type the next cell, to add it to the formula.

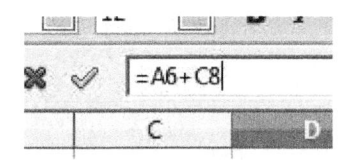

Figure 3

Step 6: Repeat **Steps 3 – 5** as necessary to complete the formula.

Step 7: When finished, press **ENTER**.

> **Note –** Be sure to press **ENTER** before clicking away from the cell. If ENTER is not pressed, each cell clicked will be added to the formula.

Growth & Assessment

1. What is an operand?

2. What is an operator?

3. Give an example of an operand.

4. All formulas begin with the pound symbol [#].

    a. TRUE

    b. FALSE

Section 2.4 – Different Types of Operators

Section Objective:

- Learn about the types of operators used in formulas.

Operations Used in Formulas

In OpenOffice Calc, there are four different types of calculation operators. Each operator is described below.

- **Arithmetic** – These operators will be used to perform basic mathematical operations such as addition, subtraction, multiplication, and division. The results for these operators are always numerical.

- **Comparison** – These operators are used to compare two values. The results for these operators will be either a value of TRUE or FALSE.

- **Text** – This operation uses the ampersand [&] to join, or concatenate, one or more text strings to produce a single piece of text. The result for this operator is text formatted in a particular sequence.

- **Reference** – These operators reference a single cell, a range (a group of adjacent cells referred to by the same name), or a reference within a list of references. The results for these operators are referenced cells, or reference names, separated by a comma, colon, or space.

The following tables cover the signs, sign meanings, and provide an example of the different operations available in each type of operator.

Arithmetic Operator

	Meaning	Example
+ (plus sign)	Addition	3+3
– (minus sign)	Subtraction	3–1
	Negation	–1
* (asterisk)	Multiplication	3*3
/ (forward slash)	Division	1
% (percent sign)	Percent	20%
^ (caret)	Exponentiation	3^2

Comparison Operator

	Meaning	Example
> (greater than sign)	Greater than	A1>B1
< (less than sign)	Less than	A1<B1
>= (greater than or equal to sign)	Greater than or equal to	A1>=B1
<= (less than or equal to sign)	Less than or equal to	A1<=B1
<> (not equal to sign)	Not equal to	A1<>B1

Text Operator

	Meaning	Example
& (ampersand)	Connects, or concatenates, two values to produce one continuous text value	"South"&"pole"

Reference Operator

	Meaning	Example
: (colon)	Range operator which produces one reference to all the cells between two references, including the two references	B5:B15
, (comma)	Union operator which combines multiple references into one reference	SUM(B5:B15,D5:D15)
(space)	Intersection operator which produces on reference to cells common to the two references	B7:D7 C6:C8

Growth & Assessment

1. What is the function of the ampersand [&]?

2. The caret [^] is used for addition.

    a. TRUE

    b. FALSE

3. Translate the following formula: B21<B4

4. A comma [,] is a union operator.

    a. TRUE

    b. FALSE

63

Section 2.5 – Using the Detective Tool

Section Objective:

- Learn how to use the Detective tool to verify data.

The Detective

The Detective is a tool used for checking which cells are used as arguments by a formula (precedents); and which cells would be affected if the source cell were to be changed (dependents). The Detective can also be used for tracing errors and locating invalid data (information in a cell that has an improper format).

This section will explain how to access the Detective tool and how to check a cell's precedents and dependencies. To explain the Detective tool, this section will use an example. Before following the steps below, create a new spreadsheet and enter the following formula into cell **C2**.

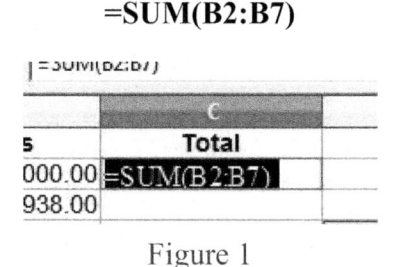

=SUM(B2:B7)

Figure 1

Locating a Cell's Precedents

The following set of steps will walk the user through using the Detective tool to look at a cell's precedents.

Step 1: Highlight cell **C2**.

Step 2: Click **Tools**, located on the Menu Bar.

Step 3: From the **Tools** drop-down menu, click **Detective** and then select **Trace Precedents**.

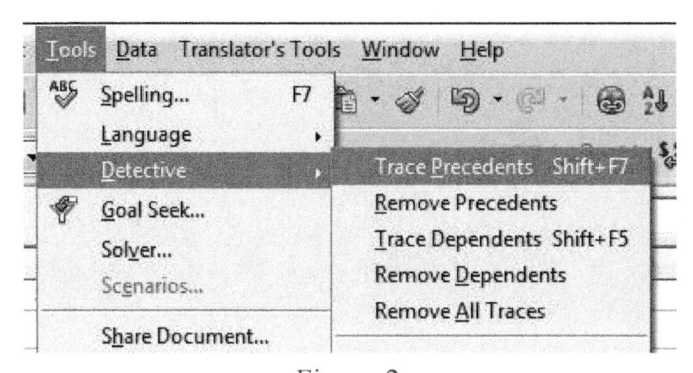

Figure 2

Once Trace Precedents has been selected, cells **B2** through **B7** will have a blue border around them. There will also be an arrow pointing to cell **C2**. The outline and arrow are displayed to show which cells are part of the formula for the calculated value shown in cell **C2**.

Figure 3

Note – The outline and arrow can be removed by going to the Tools menu. From the Tools drop-down menu click **Detective**, and then select **Remove Precedents**.

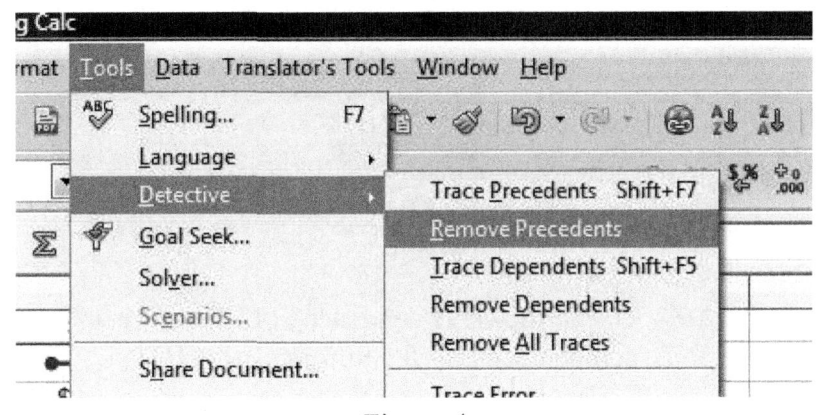

Figure 4

Locating a Cell's Dependents

Once the precedents have been located, the user can locate the cell's dependents. The following set of steps will explain how to use the Detective tool to look at a cell's dependents.

Step 1: Insert the formula **=SUM(B5:B7)** into cell **C4**.

Figure 5

Step 2: Highlight cell **B6**.

Step 3: Click **Tools**, located on the Menu Bar.

Step 4: From the **Tools** drop-down menu, click on **Detective** and then select **Trace Dependents**.

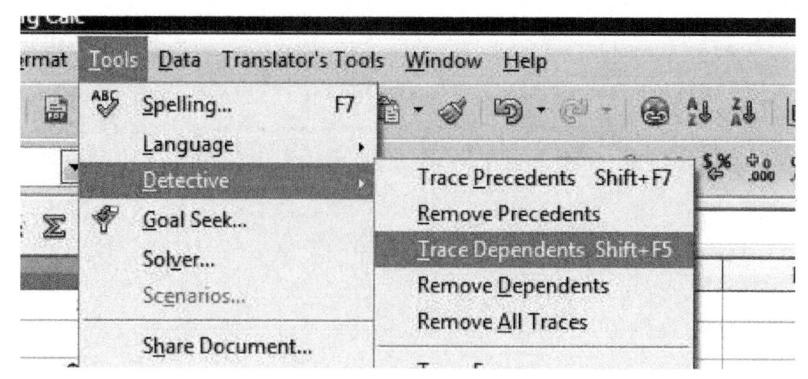

Figure 6

Once Trace Dependents has been selected, cells **B5** through **B7** will have a blue border around them. There will also be an arrow pointing to cell **C4**. The outline and arrow are displayed to show which cells are part of the formula for the calculated value shown in cell **C4**.

Figure 7

Note – Cells **B5** – **B7** are the cell's dependents. If these dependents are changed, they will affect the cell that contains the formula.

The Trace Error Function

In OpenOffice Calc, users may find that a calculation within a particular cell seems incorrect. If this happens, a user can use the Detective to trace the error. The following steps outline how this is done.

Step 1: Highlight the cell that contains the formula thought to be incorrect.

Step 2: Click **Tools**, located on the Menu Bar.

Step 3: From the **Tools** drop-down menu, click on **Detective** and then select **Trace Error**.

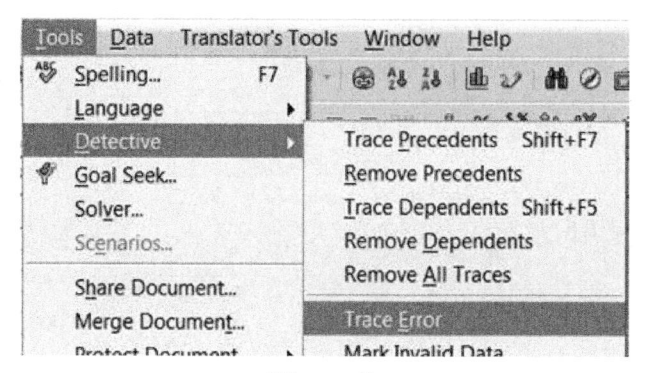

Figure 8

Once Trace Error has been selected, the Detective will outline the cells that could potentially be causing the errors within the formula.

Growth & Assessment

1. The Detective can be used to trace errors.

    a. TRUE

    b. FALSE

2. What two elements of a formula does the Detective check?

3. How can a user access the Detective feature?

Section 2.6 – Spreadsheet Auditing

Section Objective:

- Learn about spreadsheet auditing.

The Error Button

In OpenOffice Calc, various calculation errors occur. With large amounts of raw data, it is difficult for users to go through the formulas and identify which cell(s) are affecting the calculation. Calc has a feature that saves users from having to go through and examine each formula. In fact, the feature alerts users when an active cell contains an error, and it provides a description of the specific error made. The process of examining a spreadsheet for errors in formulas is referred to as auditing.

The following image is the Error button. It appears when an active cell contains an error.

Figure 1

Once a user clicks on the cell that contains the error, as stated above, a short description of the error made will be displayed in the status bar.

The following table lists the most common error codes and their meaning.

ERROR	DESCRIPTION
#####	The column is not wide enough to display the value.
#VALUE!	The formula has the wrong type of argument, for example, it has numbers where a TRUE or FALSE is required.
#NAME?	The formula contains pieces of text that Calc does not recognize; such as an incorrectly named range.
#REF!	The formula refers to a cell name that does not exist.
#DIV/0!	This error occurs when the formula attempts to divide by zero.

Growth & Assessment

1. What is the meaning of the error code "#NAME"?

2. The error code "#DIV/0" occurs when the formula attempts to divide by zero.

    a. TRUE

    b. FALSE

3. The process of examining a spreadsheet for errors in formulas is referred to as _____.

4. What error code appears when the formula refers to a cell name that does not exist?

Section 2.7 – Adding Subtotals to a Spreadsheet

Section Objective:

- Learn how to add subtotals to a spreadsheet.

Adding Subtotals to a Spreadsheet

OpenOffice Calc offers the **Subtotals** feature which allows users to break down data into subtotals. Breaking data into subtotals allows users to analyze the results in a more organized manner and allows for easier calculations. For example, if a user is looking at a spreadsheet displaying the total sales for a grocery store, the users can divide the total sales into subtotals for each department within the store, in order to easily identify which departments are the most profitable. Not only can users find the sum of a group of data, but they can also determine additional mathematical values such as Count, Average, Max, and Min; all of which help analyze the data.

Using Subtotals Feature

Step 1: Highlight the cells in the spreadsheet that contain the information that needs to be analyzed.

Step 2: Click **Data**, located on the Menu Bar.

Step 3: From the Data drop-down menu, select **Subtotals…**. The **Subtotals** dialog box will appear with the **1st Group** tab selected.

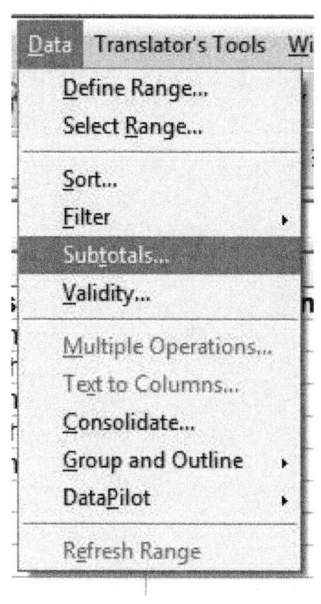

Figure 1

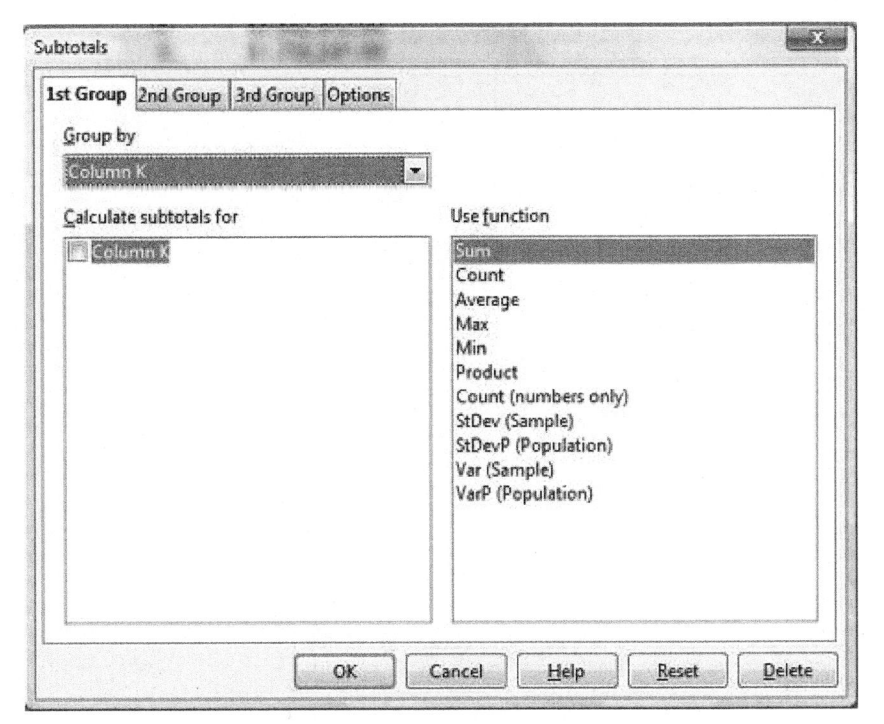

Figure 2

Step 4: Select a **Group by** column; meaning, when a user groups by a particular column, Calc will group together each distinct value within the column.

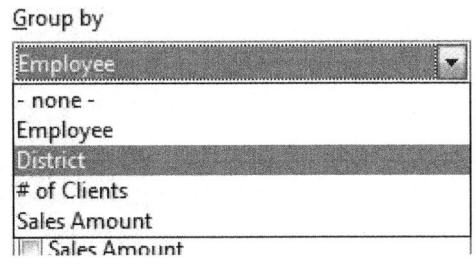

Figure 3

Step 5: Here, the user selects which columns require subtotals. Click the checkbox next to the desired values.

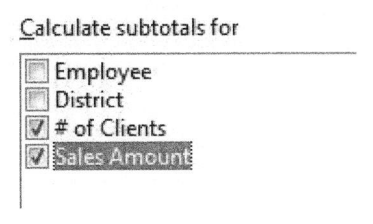

Figure 4

Step 6: Once the desired columns have been selected, the user needs to choose the function that will be used for the calculation. The available functions are listed below.

Available Functions:

- Sum
- Count
- Average
- Max
- Min
- Product
- Count (numbers only)
- StDev (Sample)
- StDevP (Population)
- Var (Sample)
- VarP (Population)

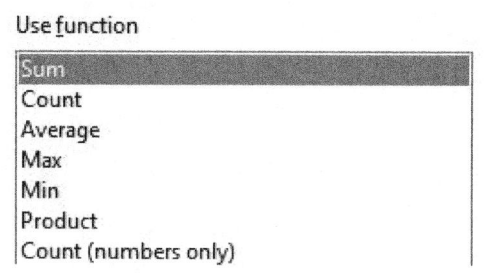

Figure 5

Step 7: Click **OK**. The subtotals will be added to the spreadsheet.

Figure 6

Deleting Subtotals

Step 1: Select a cell within the data range.

Step 2: Click **Data**, located on the Menu Bar.

Step 3: From the Data drop-down menu, select **Subtotals…**. The **Subtotals** dialog box will appear.

Step 4: Click the **Delete** button. The dialog box will close automatically and the subtotals will be removed.

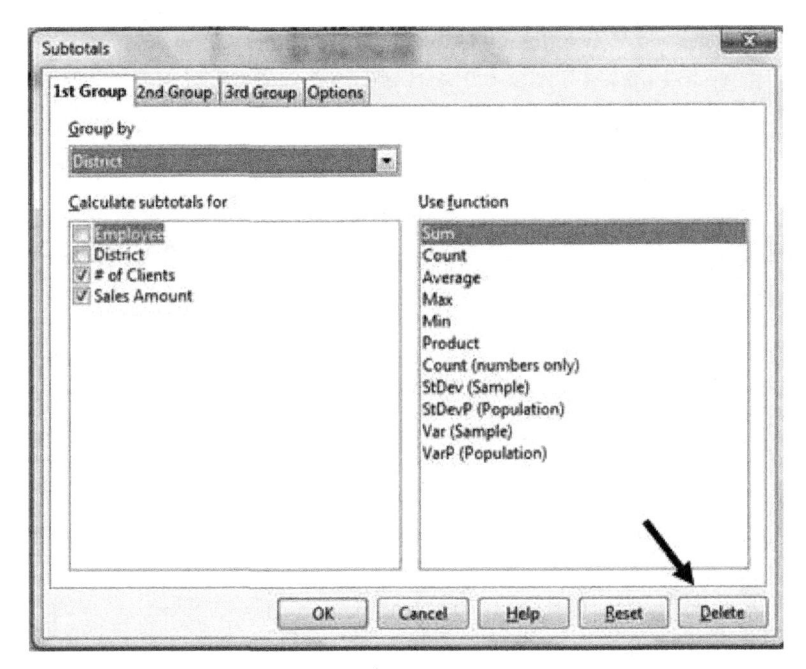

Figure 7

Growth & Assessment

1. What is the purpose of the **Subtotals** feature?

2. It is possible to find the sum of a group of data using the Subtotals feature.

    a. TRUE

    b. FALSE

3. List five of the available functions in the Subtotal feature.

Section 2.8 – Adding a Chart to a Spreadsheet

Section Objective:

- Learn how to add a chart to a spreadsheet.

Adding a Chart in Calc

OpenOffice Calc allows users to add charts to a spreadsheet. Charts are a visual representation of the data within a spreadsheet and are helpful when a user needs to display calculated results. In Calc, a basic chart is available and it can be edited and customized by using the **Chart Wizard**. The following steps outline how this is done.

Step 1: Select the data for the chart by highlighting the desired cells.

> **Note** – Include the column and row headings, these will be used to label the data within the chart.

	A	B	C
1	Team Member	2010 Sales	2011 Sales
2	John	$1,098,211.00	$30,193,282.00
3	Paul	$734,839.00	$28,173,822.00
4	George	$592,048.00	$19,293,821.00
5	Ringo	$192,831.00	$10,329,128.00
6			

Figure 1

Step 2: Click **Insert**, located on the Menu Bar.

Step 3: From the Insert drop-down menu, click **Chart…**. The **Chart Wizard** will appear with the **Chart Type** window displayed.

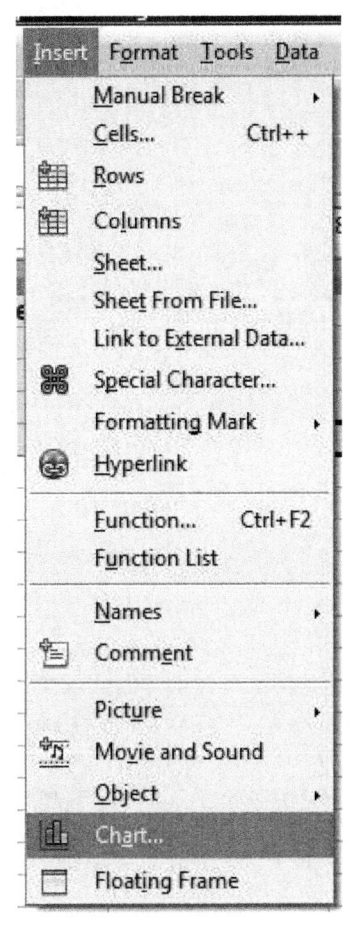

Figure 2

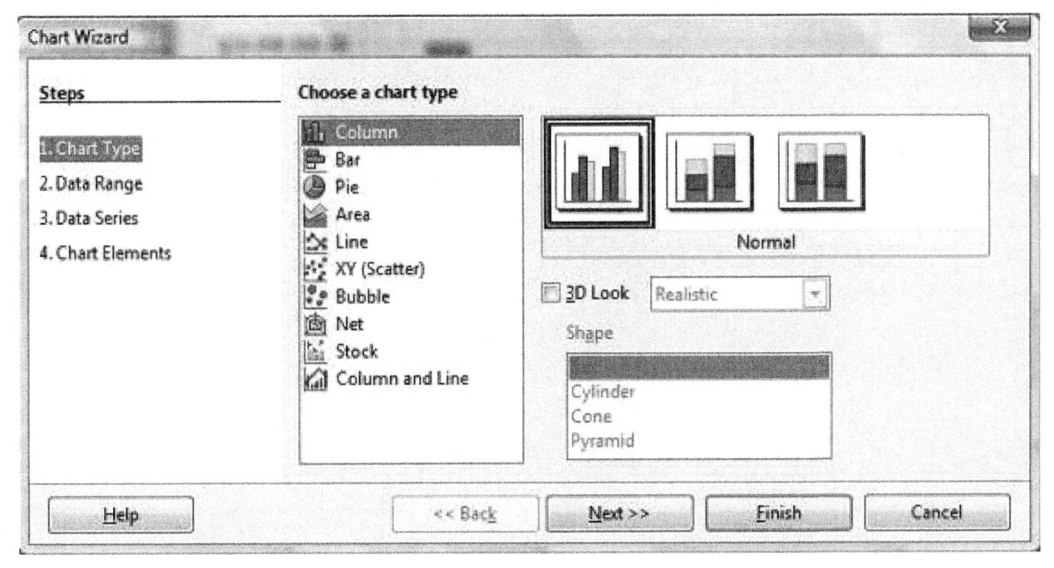

Figure 3

75

Step 4: There will be different chart categories listed along the left side of the window. Select the type of chart needed for the spreadsheet and then select the preferred chart style. The chart style options will be displayed along the right side of the window. Once the chart style has been selected, click **Next**. The Chart Wizard will bring the user to the **Data Range** window.

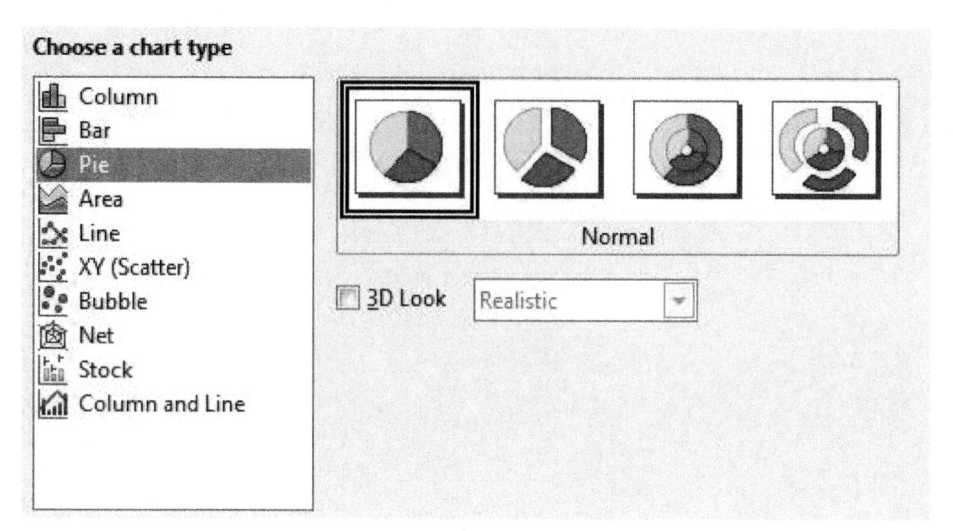

Figure 4

Step 5: Here, users have the ability to select which cells will be included in the chart. Since the cells were highlighted prior to opening the Chart Wizard, there will already be a range inserted into the textbox. After verifying that the correct cells are in the **Data Range** textbox, click **Next**. The Chart Wizard will bring the user to the **Data Series** window.

Figure 5

Step 6: The Data Series window will automatically be filled based on the highlighted cells in **Step 1**. This window inserts the data values that will be included in the chart. After verifying that the correct information has been inserted, click **Next**. The Chart Wizard will bring the user to the **Chart Elements** window.

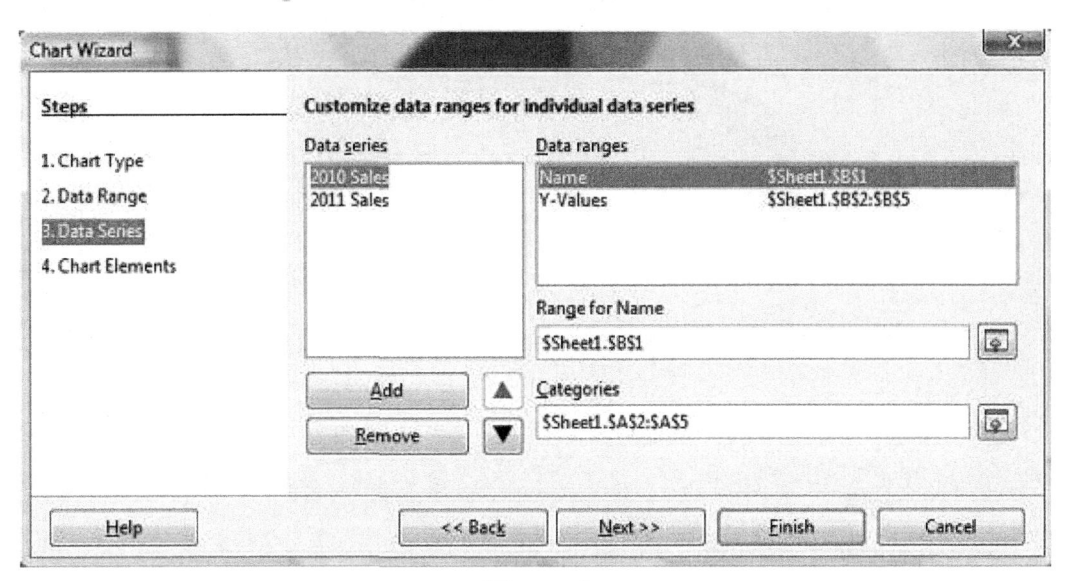

Figure 6

Step 7: The Chart Elements window is the final screen on the Chart Wizard. Here, users can name the different elements of the chart and decide where the legend, or key, will be displayed. After naming the different elements and selecting the preferred location for the legend, click **Finish**. The chart will be added to the spreadsheet.

Figure 7

77

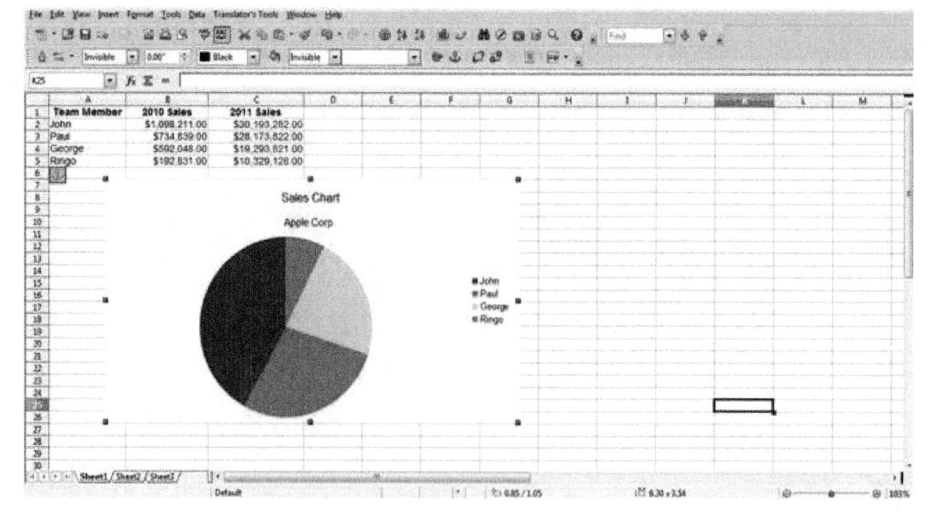

Figure 8

Modifying the Chart Type

Calc allows the user to modify the chart type after it has been added to the spreadsheet. This can be done through the **Quick Menu**. The following steps explain how this is done.

Step 1: **Right-click** on the chart. The **Quick Menu** will appear.

Step 2: From the Quick Menu, select **Chart Type....** The Chart Type dialog box will appear.

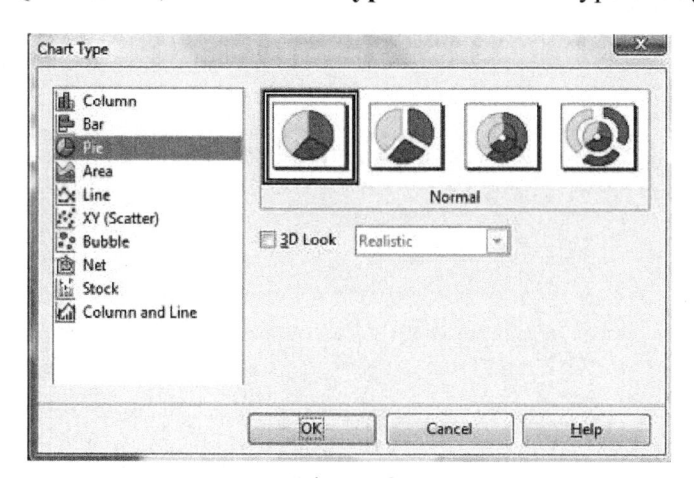

Figure 9

Step 3: Within the categories pane, select the preferred **Chart Type**.

Step 4: Once the Chart Type has been selected, choose the specific chart needed from the available options and click **OK**. The modifications will be applied to the selected chart.

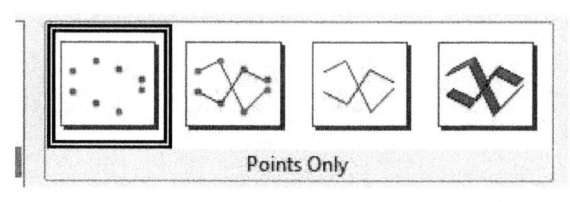

Figure 10

Moving the Chart

In OpenOffice Calc, a chart is an object on the spreadsheet. As with other objects, such as ClipArt, charts can be moved to any place on the spreadsheet. The following steps explain how this is done.

Step 1: Select the chart by clicking the left mouse button. The cursor will change into a four-headed arrow.

Step 2: Click and hold the left mouse button anywhere along the border of the chart.

Step 4: Drag the chart to the desired location.

Step 5: Once the chart is positioned over the desired location, release the mouse button. The chart will be repositioned.

Resizing the Chart

OpenOffice Calc allows users to resize a chart once it has been added to a spreadsheet. The following steps outline how this is done.

Note – When the chart is resized, the chart elements will adjust proportionally.

Step 1: Select the chart by clicking the left mouse button.

Step 2: Click and hold one of the border corners.

Step 3: While holding the left mouse button, drag the mouse to resize the chart and then release the mouse button. The chart will be resized.

Growth & Assessment

1. OpenOffice Calc does not allow users to add charts to a spreadsheet.

    a. TRUE

    b. FALSE

2. Explain how to resize a chart.

3. Basic charts can be found through the Chart Wizard.

    a. TRUE

    b. FALSE

Section 2.9 – Entering Data into Multiple Spreadsheets

Section Objective:

- Learn how to enter data into multiple spreadsheets.

Entering Data into Multiple Spreadsheets

OpenOffice Calc allows users to copy data from one spreadsheet into multiple spreadsheets. By doing this, users can perform different calculations to one set of data without disrupting the original data. The following steps outline how users can copy data to multiple spreadsheets.

Step 1: Select the tab for the spreadsheet containing the needed data.

Step 2: Hold down the **CTRL** key and click the tabs of the different spreadsheets that the data will be copied into.

   Note – Once a tab is clicked, it will be highlighted.

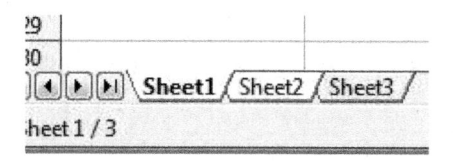

Figure 1

Step 3: Once the different spreadsheet tabs have been selected, go back to the original spreadsheet and highlight the data.

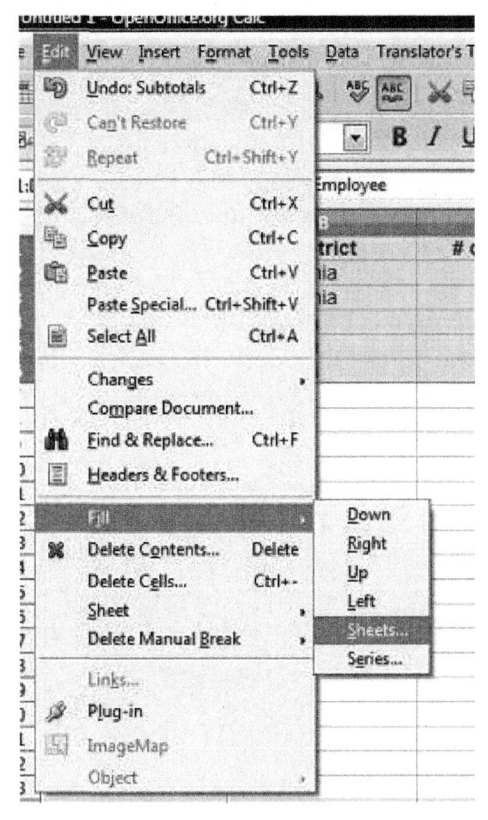

Figure 2

Step 4: Click **Edit**, located on the Menu Bar.

Step 5: From the Edit drop-down menu, click **Fill** and then select **Sheets…**. The **Fill Sheets** dialog box will appear.

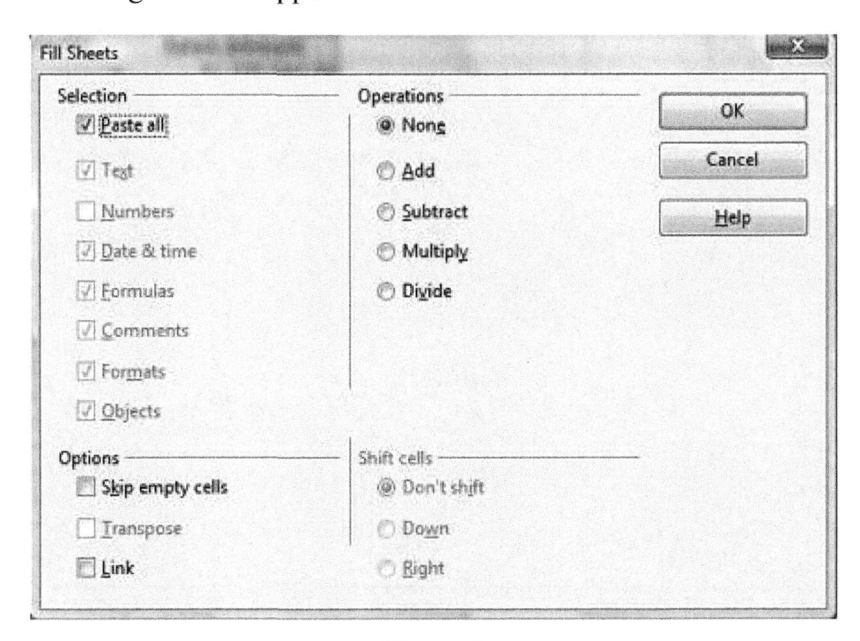

Figure 3

81

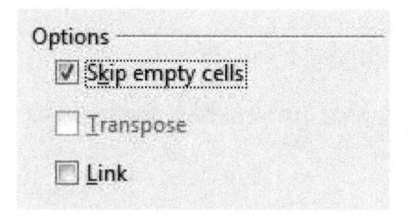

Figure 4

Step 6: Check the **Paste all** checkbox and then click **OK**. The data will appear on every spreadsheet selected in **Step 2**.

Note – If the **Skip empty cells** checkbox (located in the **Fill Sheets** dialog box) is selected, then only the highlighted cells that contain data will be moved to the other spreadsheets.

Growth & Assessment

1. OpenOffice Calc allows users to copy data from one spreadsheet into multiple spreadsheets.

    a. TRUE

    b. FALSE

2. Why is the ability to enter data from one spreadsheet into multiple spreadsheets important?

3. How do users select multiple tabs?

Section 2.10 – Using Screen Filters to Limit Data

Section Objective:

- Learn how to limit the data that appears on the screen by using an AutoFilter.

Using AutoFilters

In OpenOffice Calc, using filters will limit the rows and columns that are visible within the spreadsheet. For example, if a user created a spreadsheet that listed every sale made by a company, but only wanted to view the number of sales for widgets, then the user would set a filter to show only the rows that were widget sales. Calc allows users to create AutoFilters, which are generic filters that can be used on any type of data within a column. When accessed, they display column-specific drop-down menus from which the user can set up the filter. The following steps outline how to add a filter heading to any column in a Calc spreadsheet.

Note – The following steps cover a specific example in order to better inform the user of the uses and advantages of the AutoFilter tool.

Step 1: Create a new spreadsheet in Calc and enter the data shown in the figure below.

	A	B	C	D	E
1	First Name	Last Name	District	# of Clients	Sales Amount
2	John	John Davies	Philadelphia	9	$1,235,241.00
3	Ken	Ken Paul	Philadelphia	7	$1,234,234.00
4	Amy	Amy Hoch	Pittsburgh	16	$8,342,412.00
5	Paul	Paul Bucklin	Pittsburgh	12	$12,312,312.00
6	Josh	Josh Flaim	Pittsburgh	14	$7,463,134.00
7	John	John Riggins	Los Angeles	11	$5,832,953.00
8	Amy	Krallinger	Los Angeles	6	$981,573.00
9					

Figure 1

Step 2: Select cell **A1**, which contains the text "**Name**."

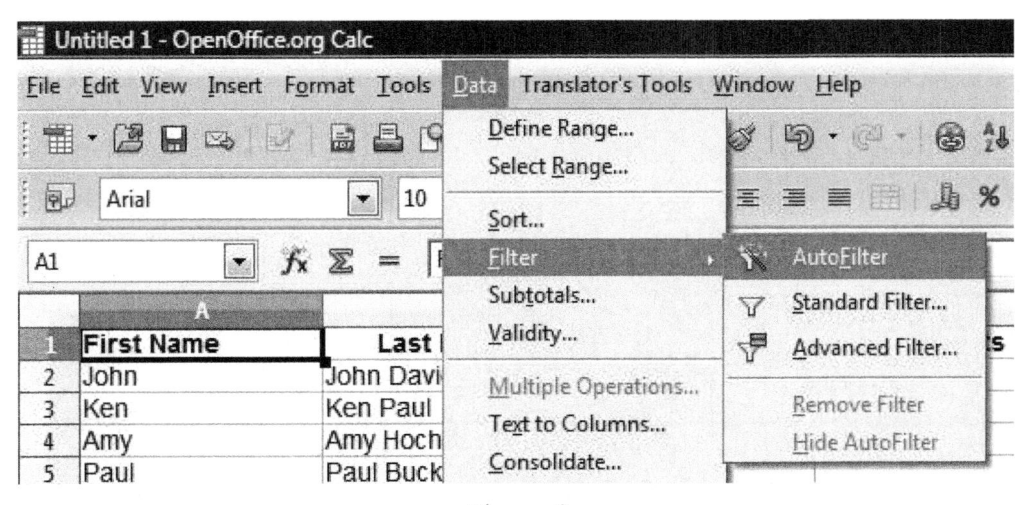

Figure 2

83

Step 3: Click Data, located on the Menu Bar.

Step 4: From the Data drop-down menu, click **Filter** and then select **AutoFilter**. An arrow will appear in the cell.

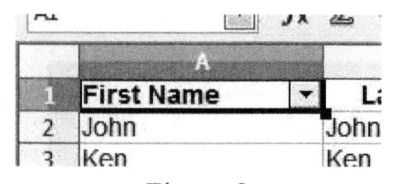

Figure 3

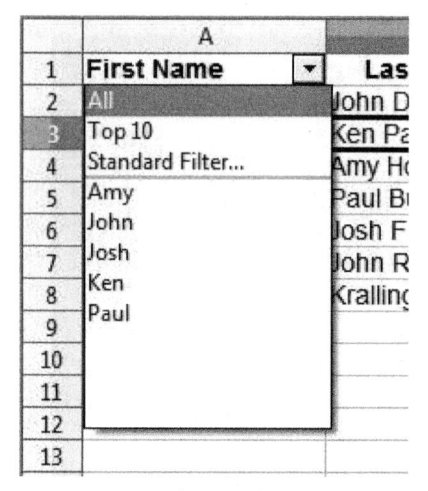

Figure 4

Step 5: In the desired column, click the arrow. The **Table Filter** drop-down list will appear.

Figure 5

The **Table Filter** drop-down list will include a submenu of column-specific records used to filter the table.

Step 6: Select the data which will be displayed. For this example, select "**Amy**." Only the records with **Amy** as the name will appear on the screen.

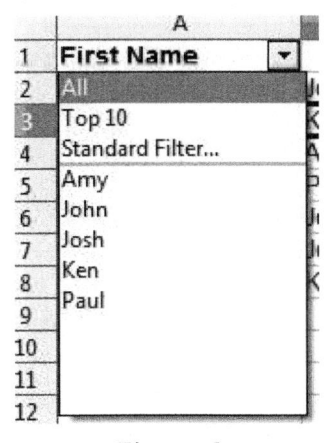

Figure 6

Note – To remove the AutoFilter from the table, click the arrow icon in the filtered column and then select **All**.

Growth & Assessment

1. What is an AutoFilter?

2. What is the purpose of using a filter in Calc?

3. Filters are applied to columns.

    a. TRUE

    b. FALSE

4. How does a user remove an AutoFilter?

Section 2.11 – Creating a Custom Filter

Section Objective:

- Learn how to create a custom filter.

Creating a Custom Filter

OpenOffice Calc allows users to create custom filters to apply to data within a spreadsheet. Filters, custom or generic, will limit the rows and columns that are visible within a spreadsheet and help users display needed information. Using a customizable Standard Filter allows users to filter a range of information and set multiple criteria for the filter. The following steps outline how to create a custom filter.

Note – The following steps cover a specific example in order to better inform the user of the uses and advantages of creating a custom filter.

Step 1: Create a new spreadsheet in Calc and enter the data shown in the figure below.

	A	B	C	D	E
1	First Name	Last Name	District	# of Clients	Sales Amount
2	John	Davies	Philadelphia	9	$1,235,241.00
3	Ken	Paul	Philadelphia	7	$1,234,234.00
4	Amy	Hoch	Pittsburgh	16	$8,342,412.00
5	Paul	Bucklin	Pittsburgh	12	$12,312,312.00
6	Josh	Flaim	Pittsburgh	14	$7,463,134.00
7	John	Riggins	Los Angeles	11	$5,832,953.00
8	Amy	Krallinger	Los Angeles	6	$981,573.00

Figure 1

Step 2: Select a cell within the spreadsheet.

Step 3: Click **Data**, located on the Menu Bar.

Step 4: From the Data drop-down menu, click **Filter** and then select **Standard Filter**. The **Standard Filter** dialog box will appear.

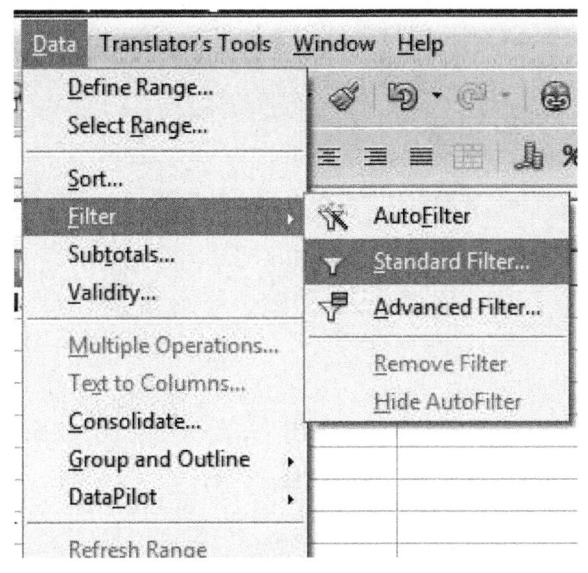

Figure 2

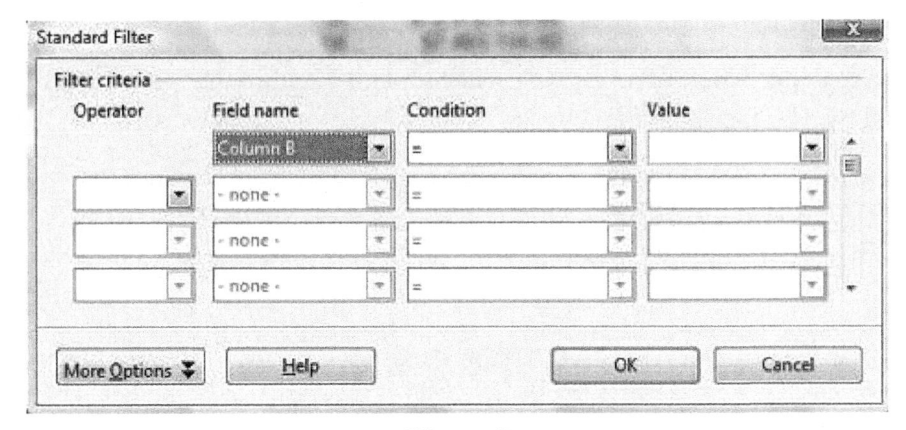

Figure 3

Step 5: In the **Field Name** drop-down list, select the first field to filter the data by. For this example, choose "**Name**."

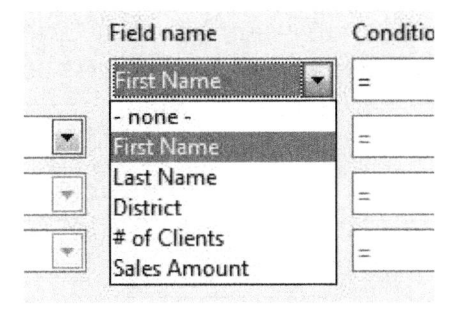

Figure 4

87

Step 6: In the **Condition** drop-down list, select the operator to filter the data by. For this example, choose "=."

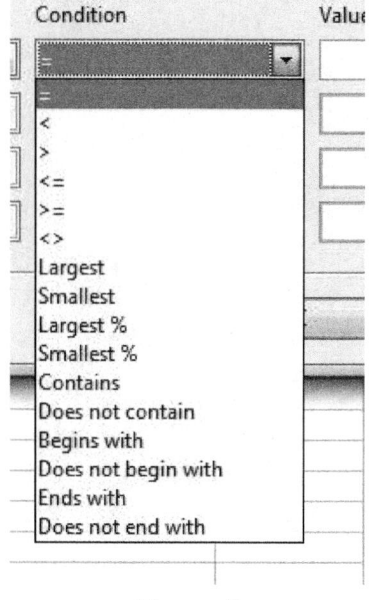

Figure 5

Step 7: In the **Value** drop-down list, select which value within the spreadsheet to filter the data by. For this example, choose "**Chris**."

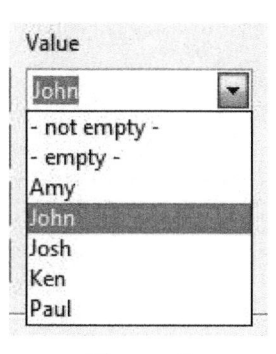

Figure 6

Step 8: To add a second criterion to the filter, the user needs to choose a value in the **Operator** drop-down list. For this example, choose the "**And**" value. This means that both criteria must be met for the value to be shown in the spreadsheet.

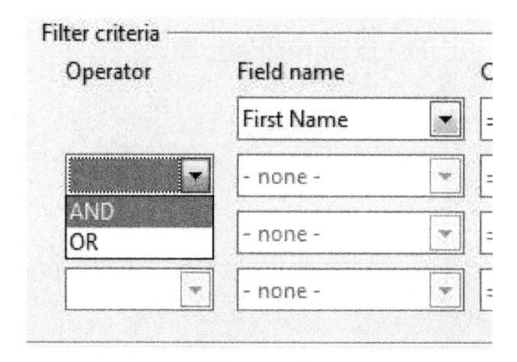

Figure 7

Note – By selecting the **Or** value from the **Operator** drop-down list, any data that matched one or more selected criteria would be shown within the spreadsheet.

Step 9: In the **Field** drop-down menu, choose "**Items Sold**," and in the **Condition** drop-down menu, select ">."

Step 10: In the **Value** textbox type "**15**" and then click **OK**. The filter will be applied to the spreadsheet.

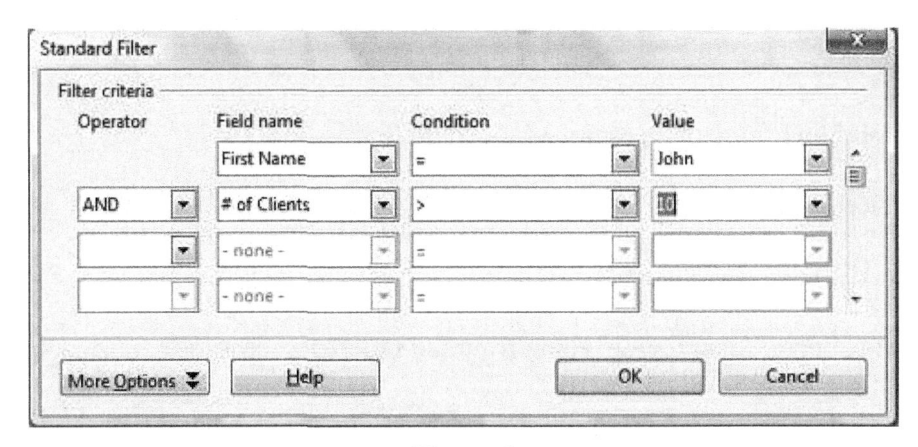

Figure 8

Removing a Custom Filter

OpenOffice Calc allows users to remove a custom filter once it has been created. The following steps outline how this is done.

Step 1: Select any cell, within the spreadsheet, that the filter was applied to.

Step 2: Click **Data**, located on the Menu Bar.

Step 3: From the Data drop-down menu, click **Filter** and then select **Remove Filter**. The filter will be removed and all of the data contained within the spreadsheet will be displayed.

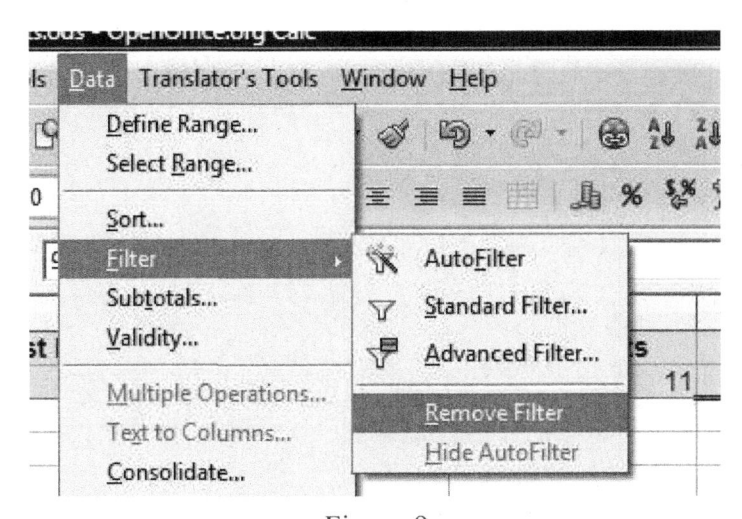

Figure 9

Growth & Assessment

1. A custom filter can only limit rows within a spreadsheet.

    a. TRUE

    b. FALSE

2. What does a customizable Standard Filter allow a user to do?

3. Custom filters cannot be removed.

    a. TRUE

    b. FALSE

4. What happens when the **Or** value from the **Operator** drop-down list is selected?

Section 2.12 – Working With Advanced Filters

Section Objective:

- Learn how to create an Advanced Filter.

Creating an Advanced Filter

The OpenOffice Calc **Advanced Filter** is similar to the AutoFilter in the sense that it filters a list based on the criteria specified by the user; however, the Advanced Filter uses a different mechanism to define the criteria used.

The Advanced Filter defines the criteria within the actual Calc spreadsheet. To use an Advanced Filter, users must set up a criteria matrix using the same columns and headers as the main database. Each row of the criteria matrix corresponds to a condition, which will be applied to the spreadsheet when filtering. All criteria in the same row will be treated as **AND** conditions, while all criteria in different rows are treated as **OR** conditions.

Note – The following steps cover a specific example in order to better inform the user of the uses and advantages of creating an Advanced Filter. Before beginning the steps, create a new Calc spreadsheet that contains the data in the figure shown below.

	A	B	C	D	E
1	First Name	Last Name	District	# of Clients	Sales Amount
2	John	Davies	Philadelphia	9	$1,235,241.00
3	Ken	Paul	Philadelphia	7	$1,234,234.00
4	Amy	Hoch	Pittsburgh	16	$8,342,412.00
5	Chris	Mitchell	Pittsburgh	12	$12,312,312.00
6	Josh	Flaim	Pittsburgh	14	$7,463,134.00
7	John	Riggins	Los Angeles	11	$5,832,953.00
8	Amy	Krallinger	Los Angeles	6	$981,573.00

Figure 1

Steps for Setting up an Advanced Filter:

Step 1: Copy the headings in cells **A1** through **E1** into cells **A10** through **E10**.

	A	B	C	D	E
1	First Name	Last Name	District	# of Clients	Sales Amount
2	John	Davies	Philadelphia	9	$1,235,241.00
3	Ken	Paul	Philadelphia	7	$1,234,234.00
4	Amy	Hoch	Pittsburgh	16	$8,342,412.00
5	Chris	Mitchell	Pittsburgh	12	$12,312,312.00
6	Josh	Flaim	Pittsburgh	14	$7,463,134.00
7	John	Riggins	Los Angeles	11	$5,832,953.00
8	Amy	Krallinger	Los Angeles	6	$981,573.00
9					
10	First Name	Last Name	District	# of Clients	Sales Amount
11					
12					

Figure 2

Step 2: Set up the criteria to only select rows where the District is equal to Pittsburgh. This is done by entering the text "**Pittsburgh**" into cell **C11**.

District
Pittsburgh

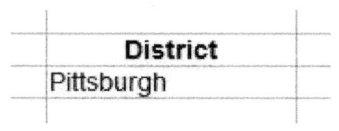

Figure 3

Step 3: In the same row as above, set up the criteria to only select rows where the sales exceeded $5,000,000. This is done by entering the text "**>5000000**" into cell **E11**.

Note – With **And** clauses, added criteria needs to be set up on the same row as the previous criteria. With **Or** clauses, added criteria needs to be set up in a different row. For this example, the Sales criteria would be entered into cell **D12**.

Sales Amount
>5000000

Figure 4

	A	B	C	D	E
1	First Name	Last Name	District	# of Clients	Sales Amount
2	John	Davies	Philadelphia	9	$1,235,241.00
3	Ken	Paul	Philadelphia	7	$1,234,234.00
4	Amy	Hoch	Pittsburgh	16	$8,342,412.00
5	Chris	Mitchell	Pittsburgh	12	$12,312,312.00
6	Josh	Flaim	Pittsburgh	14	$7,463,134.00
7	John	Riggins	Los Angeles	11	$5,832,953.00
8	Amy	Krallinger	Los Angeles	6	$981,573.00
9					
10	First Name	Last Name	District	# of Clients	Sales Amount
11			Pittsburgh		>5000000
12					

Figure 5

Steps for Activating an Advanced Filter:

In OpenOffice Calc, the Advanced Filter matrix must be set up before activating the Advanced Filter because the matrix specifies the criteria on which the data is filtered. Now that the matrix has been created, the Advanced Filter can be activated. The following steps outline how this is done.

Step 1: Highlight the cells which the filter will be applied to.

> **Note** – Do not highlight the cells that contain the **Criteria Matrix**.

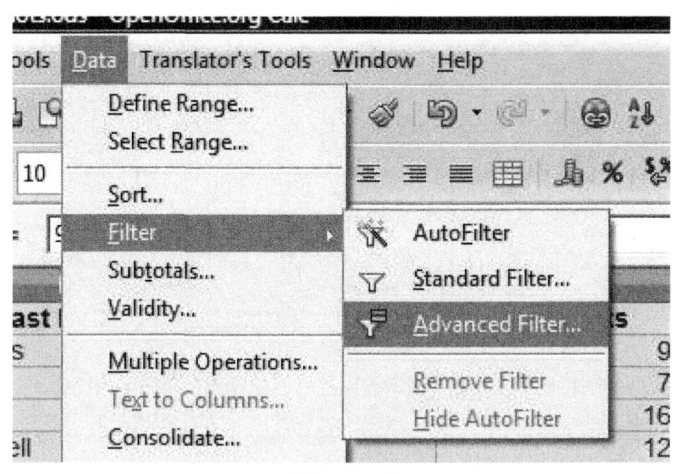

Figure 6

Step 2: Click **Data**, located on the Menu Bar.

Step 3: From the Data drop-down menu, click **Filter** and then select **Advanced Filter…**. The **Advanced Filter** dialog box will appear.

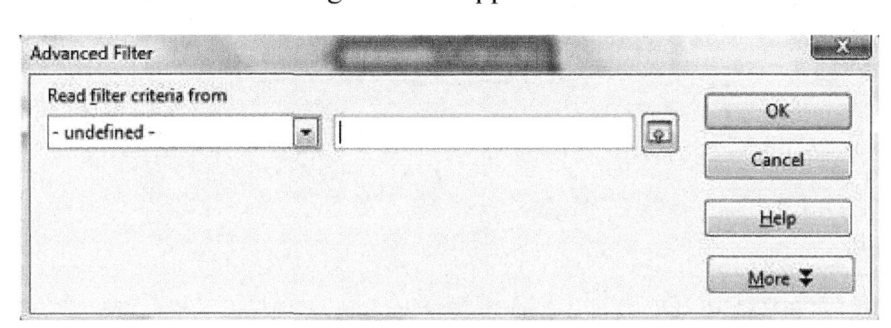

Figure 7

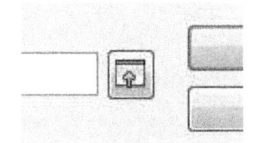

Figure 8

Step 4: Click the **Shrink** button to shrink the dialog box enough to view the Criteria Matrix.

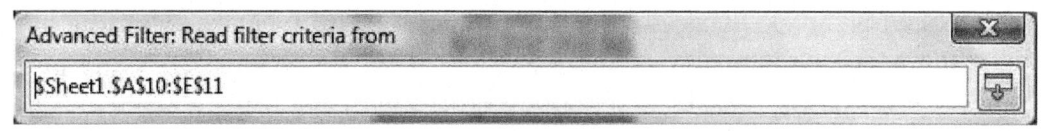

Figure 9

Step 5: Highlight the **Criteria Matrix**. This will enter the range into the **Advanced Filter** textbox.

Figure 10

Step 6: Click the **Shrink Button** once again to return to the full **Advanced Filter** dialog box.

Step 7: Click **OK**. The filter will be applied to the spreadsheet data.

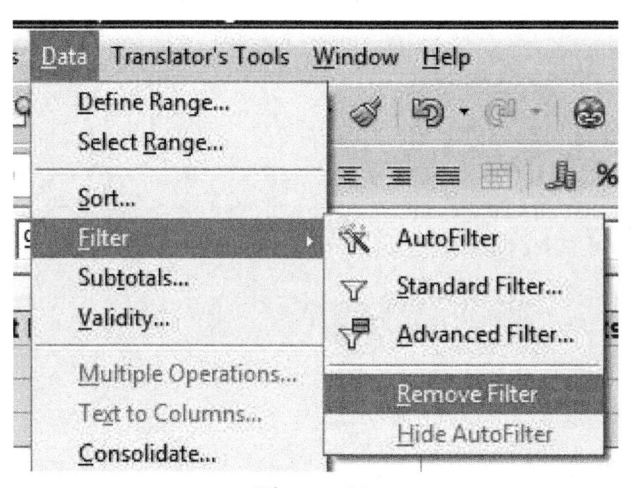

Figure 11

Note – This section had the Criteria Matrix set up next to the data within the spreadsheet for teaching purposes. When creating an Advanced Filter in the future, it is best to place the matrix in cells that are far removed from the spreadsheet data.

Removing an Advanced Filter

An Advanced Filter is removed the same way as other filters are removed in OpenOffice Calc. The following steps outline how this is done.

Step 1: Select any cell within the spreadsheet that the filter was applied to.

Step 2: Click **Data**, located on the Menu Bar.

Step 3: From the Data drop-down menu, click **Filter** and then select **Remove Filter**. The filter will be removed and all of the data contained within the spreadsheet will be displayed.

Growth & Assessment

1. Advanced Filter is similar to the AutoFilter.

    a. TRUE

    b. FALSE

2. What does the **Shrink** button do?

3. What condition is all of the criteria within the same row treated as?

4. What condition is all of the criteria within different rows treated as?

Section 2.13 – Getting Running Totals

Section Objective:

- Learn how to generate running totals for the values of a group of cells.

Accessing Running Totals

OpenOffice Calc allows users to track mathematical calculations, or running totals, at the bottom of the application's window while entering data into the spreadsheet. This is helpful when trying to access information quickly without having to create formulas. The following steps explain how users can access and display this information.

Step 1: Open a previously save spreadsheet containing data.

Step 2: Select a group of cells that contain data.

	A
1	5
2	7
3	323
4	9
5	78
6	32
7	796
8	32
9	68
10	

Figure 1

	A
1	5
2	7
3	323
4	9
5	78
6	32
7	796
8	32
9	68
10	

Figure 2

Step 3: Right-click the **Status Bar** at the bottom of the application's window. The **Status Bar** menu will appear.

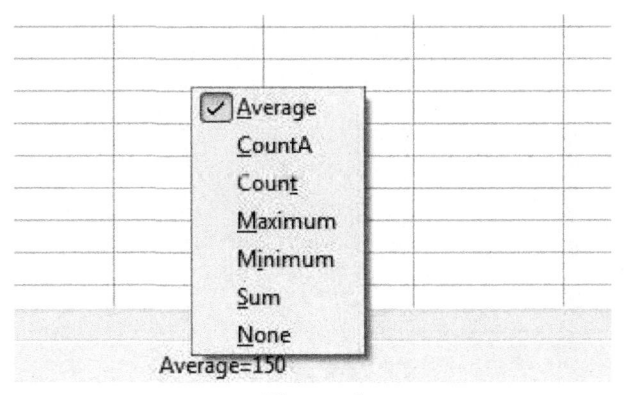

Figure 3

Step 4: Select the desired running totals. Below is a list of the available mathematical calculations the Status bar offers.

Available Calculations:

- Average
- CountA
- Count
- Maximum
- Minimum
- Sum
- None

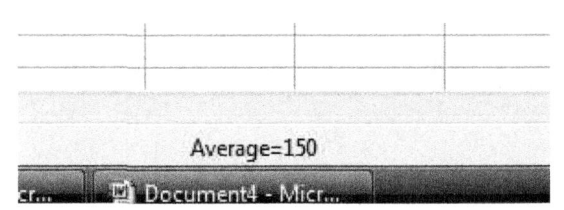

Figure 4

Growth & Assessment

1. When would running totals be useful?

2. List two available calculation options found within the Status bar.

3. Running totals will change when the data within the cells changes.

    a. TRUE

    b. FALSE

97

Section 2.14 – Improving Accuracy of Spreadsheets

Section Objective:

- Learn validation techniques to improve the accuracy of spreadsheets.

Validation Techniques

In OpenOffice Calc there are various validation techniques that can be used when working with data. Users can set up validation requirements for a single cell or an entire spreadsheet depending on the need. This is helpful when a user creates a spreadsheet that will be used by multiple people because by setting up validation requirements, only valid information, specified by the spreadsheet creator, will be accepted in a particular cell. For example, if a student wants to collect their classmates' names and birthdates, and enter the information into a Calc spreadsheet, the student can set up the validation requirements in a way that wouldn't allow the students' information to be entered incorrectly. The student could restrict numerical entries within the "name" column and restrict letters from the "birth date" column. The student could even restrict all entries within other columns so the only two columns that can accept data entries are the two needed columns. This would ensure that the data isn't entered in the wrong column.

Validation requirements are also helpful when a user collects a large amount of data. Many times when entering large amounts of data into a spreadsheet, a user might enter data incorrectly which would later affect the analysis and results, so by creating a list of valid entries, the user can lower inaccuracies and increase the data's validity. The following steps outline how a user can set up a drop-down list of validation requirements for any given cell.

Step 1: Create a new Calc spreadsheet and select any cell. This cell will be used to create a validation drop-down list.

Step 2: Click Data, located on the Menu Bar.

Step 3: IFrom in the Data drop-down menu, click **Validity…**. The **Validity** dialog box will appear.

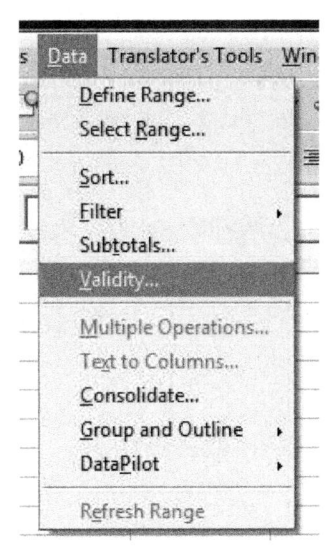

Figure 1

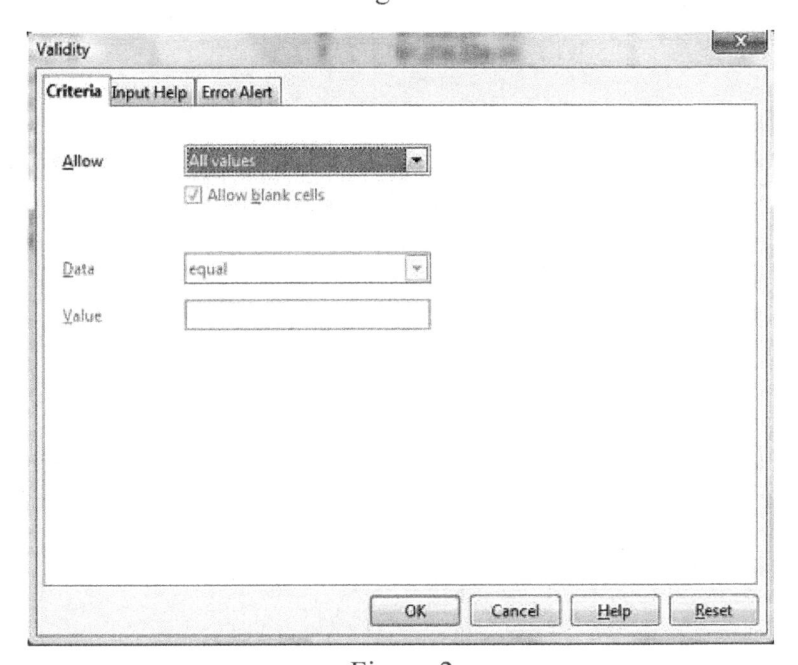

Figure 2

Step 4: In the **Allow** drop-down menu, select the valid entry types; such as, decimal entries, alphabetic characters, whole numbers, etc…

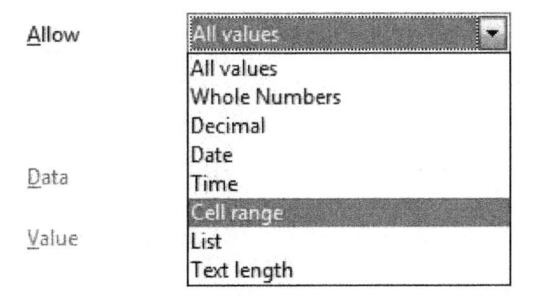

Figure 3

99

Step 5: In the **Data** drop-down menu, specify the validity test. These options vary depending on the validation type selected in the Allow drop-down menu.

> **Note** – Depending on the type of validation, a value may be needed for the validity test. For example, if "**whole numbers**" was selected in the **Allow** drop-down menu, and "**greater than**" was selected in the **Data** drop-down menu, a numerical value would be needed to test the validity of an entry.

Step 6: If the validation test requires a value, specify the needed value in the **Value** textbox.

> **Note** – To specify whether the cell can be left blank, select or clear the **Allow blank cells** checkbox.

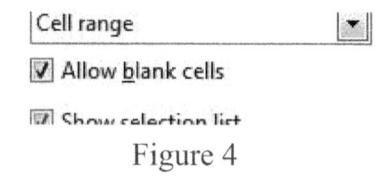

Figure 4

Step 7: Once the type of validation requirements have been set up, click **OK**. The specified validity requirements will be applied to the selected cell.

> **Note** – As stated above, cells can stop, warn, or provide the user with an error message when invalid data is entered into a cell. These options are provided within the **Error Alert** tab in the **Validity** dialog box.

Growth & Assessment

1. There are many validation types.

    a. TRUE

    b. FALSE

2. What can be selected within the **Allow** drop-down menu?

3. Cells can stop, warn, or provide the user with an error message when invalid data is entered into a cell.

    a. TRUE

    b. FALSE

Section 2.15 – Sorting Data

Section Objective:

- Learn how to sort data.

Sorting Data

OpenOffice Calc provides users with the **Sort Command** which arranges spreadsheet data by text (i.e., A to Z, Z to A), numbers (i.e., smallest to largest, largest to smallest), dates, or times (oldest to newest, newest to oldest). The following steps outline how to sort data within a spreadsheet.

Sorting by an Ascending or Descending Order

OpenOffice Calc allows users to easily sort by an **Ascending** or **Descending** order. The following steps outline how this is done.

Step 1: Open a previously saved Calc spreadsheet.

	A	B	C	D	E
1	First Name	Last Name	District	# of Clients	Sales Amount
2	John	Davies	Philadelphia	9	$1,235,241.00
3	Ken	Paul	Philadelphia	7	$1,234,234.00
4	Amy	Hoch	Pittsburgh	16	$8,342,412.00
5	Chris	Mitchell	Pittsburgh	12	$12,312,312.00
6	Josh	Flaim	Pittsburgh	14	$7,463,134.00
7	John	Riggins	Los Angeles	11	$5,832,953.00
8	Amy	Krallinger	Los Angeles	6	$981,573.00

Figure 1

Step 2: Select a cell within a column containing multiple rows of data.

Step 3: From the **Formatting Toolbar**, click either the **Ascending** or **Descending** button to sort the data. Once clicked, the data within the selected column will be sorted.

Ascending   Descending

Figure 2

101

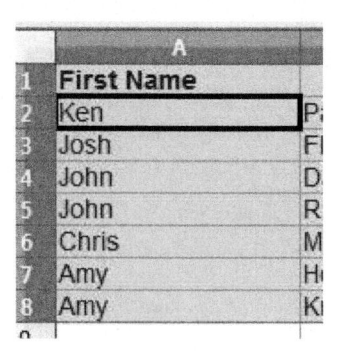

Figure 3

Note – When sorting in Calc using the toolbar, the value in the selected cell is treated as a heading and will not be sorted with the rest of the data.

Sorting through the Sort Dialog Box

OpenOffice Calc allows users to create multi-level sorts that meet a variety of specifications. The following steps outline how this is done.

Step 1: Open a previously saved Calc spreadsheet.

Figure 4

Step 2: Select any cell within the spreadsheet.

Step 3: Click **Data**, located on the Menu Bar.

Step 4: From in the **Data** drop-down menu, click **Sort…**. The **Sort** dialog box will appear.

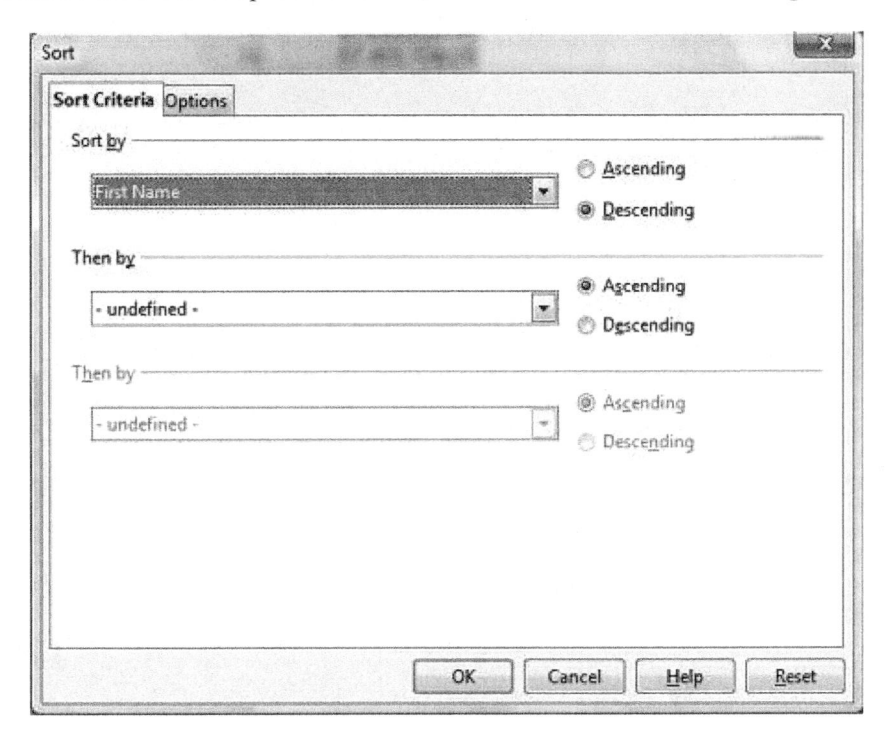

Figure 5

Step 5: In the **Sort By** drop-down menu, select which column the sort will be applied to.

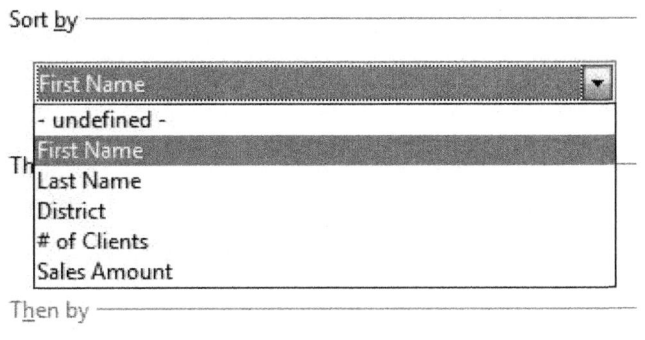

Figure 6

Step 6: To the right of the **Sort By** drop-down menu, select whether the data is to be sorted in an **Ascending** or **Descending** order.

Figure 7

Step 7: In the **Then By** drop-down menu, select a secondary column to sort by meaning, if there are duplicate values in column 1, the user can set secondary criteria.

Figure 8

Step 8: Click **OK**. The data will be sorted based on the options selected.

Note – It is possible to not include the column or row heading when setting a sort through the **Sort** dialog box. To do this, users must first click the **Options** tab and then uncheck the checkbox next to **Range Contains Column Labels**.

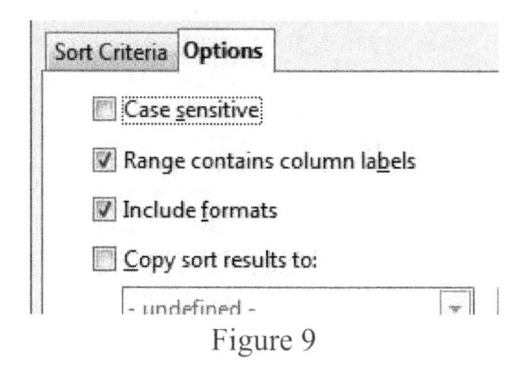

Figure 9

Growth & Assessment

1. Where are the Ascending and Descending buttons located?

2. What is one option in the **Sort By** drop-down menu?

3. Calc only allows users to sort by number.

   a. TRUE

   b. FALSE

Unit Three

Section 3.1 – Changing the Appearance of a Document   108

Section 3.2 – Types of Tools on the Formatting Toolbar   111

Section 3.3 – Using Font Color and Size Control Tools   114

Section 3.4 – Using the Borders Button   117

Section 3.5 – Using the Fill Button   121

Section 3.6 – Exporting Spreadsheets to a PDF   125

Section 3.7 – Applying Formatting to Numbers   132

Section 3.8 – Adding Date and Time   135

Section 3.9 – Using Headers and Footers   137

Section 3.10 – Formatting Cells Using Conditional Formatting   141

Section 3.11 – Creating a Customized Conditional Formatting Style   145

Section 3.12 – Editing Conditional Formatting Styles   151

Section 3.13 – Positioning Data on a Printout   155

Section 3.14 – Defining Print Area   160

Section 3.15 – Printing Ranges of Cells   163

Section 3.1 – Changing the Appearance of a Document

Section Objective:

- Learn why changing the appearance of a document is important.

Changing the Appearance of a Document in Calc

OpenOffice Calc allows users to change the appearance of a spreadsheet. The careful use of color, shading, borders, and fonts doesn't only add visual appeal; it also allows the user to better organize the data. Organizing the data allows viewers to locate the results and other important information quickly and easily. This section will explain how to access these various formatting options and explain why it is important for users to change the appearance of their spreadsheet.

To better organize the spreadsheet and make it more visually appealing, the user will need to adjust the format of the spreadsheet, specifically the alignment, color, borders, and shading. Calc offers two ways of formatting a spreadsheet; the user can use tools found on the **Formatting Toolbar**, or the user can go through the **Format Cells** dialog box. The following steps outline how to access both of these options.

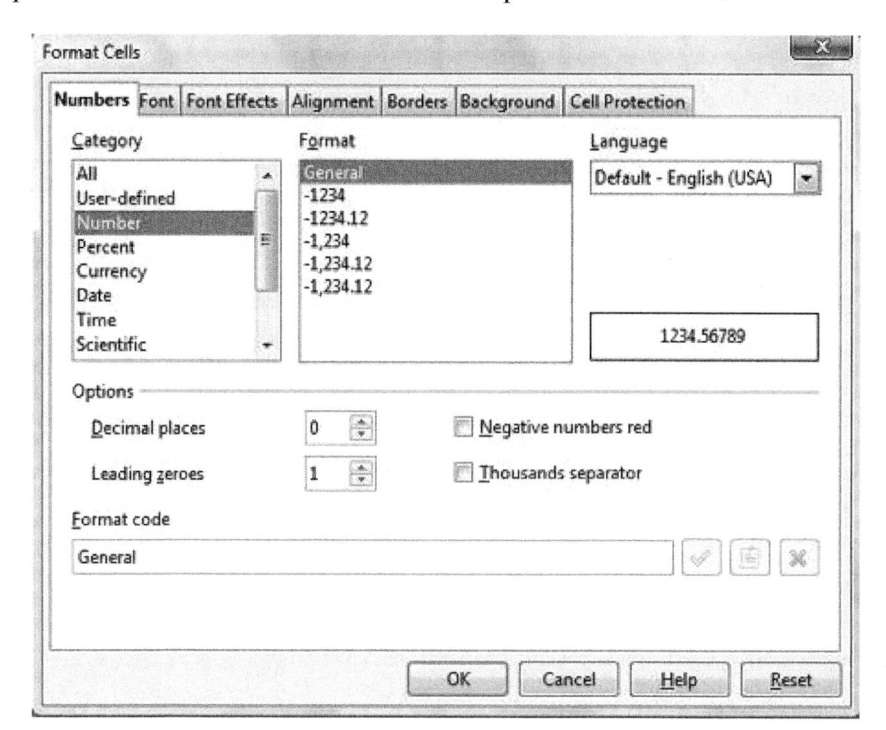

Figure 1

Steps for Accessing the Format Cells Dialog Box:

Step 1: Click **Format**, located on the Menu Bar.

Step 2: From in the Format drop-down menu, click **Cells**. The **Format Cells** dialog box will appear.

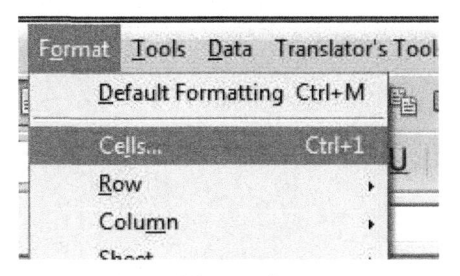

Figure 2

Step 3: Click the **Font** or the **Font Effects** tab to find the **Font Formatting Tools**. Here, users have the ability to select from various formatting options for the spreadsheet.

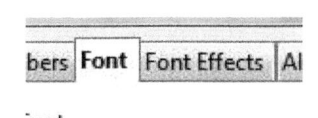

Figure 3

Steps for Accessing the Formatting Toolbar:

OpenOffice Calc allows users to modify the appearance of a spreadsheet through the tools found on the **Formatting Toolbar**. View the figure below to identify which buttons to use when formatting a spreadsheet.

Figure 4

Customizing the Font and Color of the text is one way to draw attention and better display the results within a spreadsheet. Some of the font and color options made available to the user are listed below.

- **Font Style** – This selection determines the font of the text that will be entered into the spreadsheet. Arial is the standard font for new spreadsheets.

- **Font Size** – This selection determines the size of the Font. Font Size is measured in points. The default size for a Calc spreadsheet is 10 point, but the user has the ability to adjust this size from 1 point to 409 point.

- **Font Attributes** – This selection determines the font attributes. The attributes that a user can add to the selected font are *italics*, underline, and **bold**.

- **Font Color** – This selection determines the color of the text. Black is the default color for a Calc spreadsheet; however, the application provides hundreds of colors to choose from.

Growth & Assessment

1. Give an example of a font attribute?

2. Formatting the border is one way to give a spreadsheet visual appeal.

    a. TRUE

    b. FALSE

3. What is the largest font size in Calc?

Section 3.2 – Types of Tools on the Formatting Toolbar

Section Objective:

- Learn about the tools available on the formatting toolbar.

The Formatting Toolbar

The **Formatting Toolbar** found in OpenOffice Calc gives the user the ability to modify the look of the data within a spreadsheet without having to navigate away from the spreadsheet. This section will provide an overview of the Font, Alignment, Number, and Cell formatting controls found on the **Formatting Toolbar**.

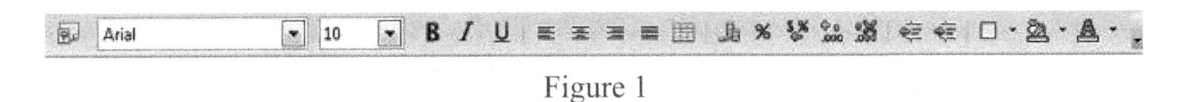

Figure 1

The following **Font** controls can be used to modify the look of the text within a Calc spreadsheet.

Figure 2

- **Font Type** – Use the **Font Type** drop-down menu to choose the type of font that will be used.

- **Font Size** – Use the **Font Size** drop-down menu to select the size of the font that will be used.

- **Font Attributes** – Use the **Typeface** buttons to add bold, italics, or an underline to the text.

The following **Alignment** controls can be used to modify the alignment of text or numbers found within the cells of a spreadsheet.

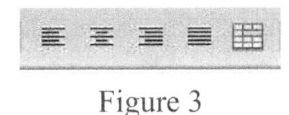

Figure 3

- **Alignment Buttons** – Use the **Left Justified**, **Right Justified**, **Center Justified**, and **Justified** buttons to adjust where the data is positioned within the cells.

- **Merge Button** – Use the **Merge Button** to merge multiple cells into a single cell.

The following buttons can only be used with numerical data. These are used to identify the different types of numbers used within a spreadsheet.

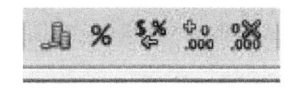

Figure 4

- **Currency Button** – Use this button to change the formatting of the numerical data to the currency data type. This type will place a dollar sign at the beginning of the number and two decimal places behind the number. This is an important formatting option when working with data used for accounting, finance, and other types of subjects that deal with currency.

- **Percentage Button** – The Percentage button will change any number into a percentage. It does this by multiplying the number a in cell by 100 and adding a percent sign to the cell. For example if the cell contained the number .45, the number after hitting the Percentage button would be 45.00%.

- **Standard Button** – Click on this button to return any formatted text back to the standard formatting. The standard formatting right aligns the number with no decimal places.

- **Add or Remove Decimal Place Buttons** – These buttons add and remove a decimal place from the number. This is helpful when working with improper fractions or other numerical values that require rounding.

The following buttons will move the entire contents of a cell to the left or right, by increasing or decreasing the indent.

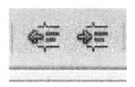

Figure 5

- **Increase Indent** – Click this button to shift the data within a cell to the right.

- **Decrease Indent** – Click this button to shift the data within a cell to the left.

Note – A user can only shift the text within a cell to the left until the text reaches the left border.

The final set of buttons is used to modify the border and color(s) of both the cells and text.

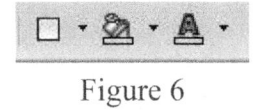

Figure 6

- **Borders** – Click the arrow next to this button to view the different types of borders that can be applied to the lines of the highlighted cell(s).

- **Background Color** – Click the arrow next to this button to view the different colors that can be applied to the background of the spreadsheet.

- **Font Color** – This menu is used to select the color of the text within the cells.

Growth & Assessment

1. What does the Currency Button do?

2. Calc allows users to change the background color.

    a. TRUE

    b. FALSE

3. Clicking the Increase Indent Button will shift the cells to the left.

    a. TRUE

    b. FALSE

4. The Alignment Buttons allow users to change the position of the text in what four ways?

Section 3.3 – Using Font Color and Size Control Tools

Section Objective:

- Learn how to use the Font Color and Size Control.

Font Color and Size Control

In OpenOffice Calc, users have the ability to change the look of the text through changing the font, size, and color from the Toolbar and the Format Cells dialog box. This section will explain how to utilize both of these options and modify the text within a spreadsheet.

These first steps will outline how to change the format of a spreadsheet by using the Toolbar.

Formatting the Text Using the Toolbar

Step 1: Create a new Calc spreadsheet and enter text into any cell. Once the text has been entered, select the cell.

Step 2: Select a different **Font Size**. This is done by locating the **Font Size** drop-down list on the Toolbar. The size of the text within the selected cell will adjust once the preferred size has been selected.

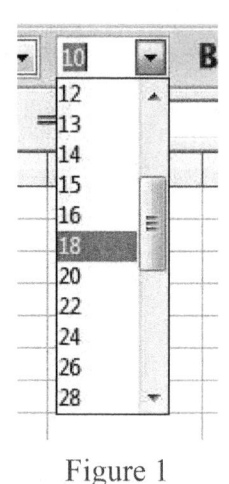

Figure 1

Step 3: Select a different **Font Color**. This is done by locating the Font Color on the Toolbar and clicking the arrow next to the Font Color button. Once the arrow has been clicked, a variety of colors will be available for the user to choose from.

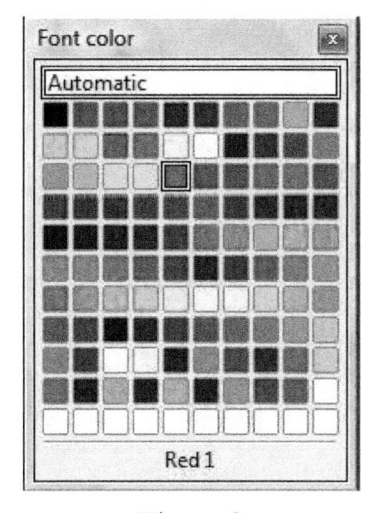

Figure 2

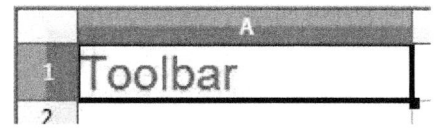

Figure 3

Formatting the Text Using the Format Cells Dialog Box

Step 1: Create a new Calc spreadsheet and enter text into any cell. Once the text has been entered, select the cell.

Step 2: Click **Format**, located on the Menu Bar.

Step 3: From the Format drop-down menu, click **Cells…**. The **Format Cells** dialog box will appear.

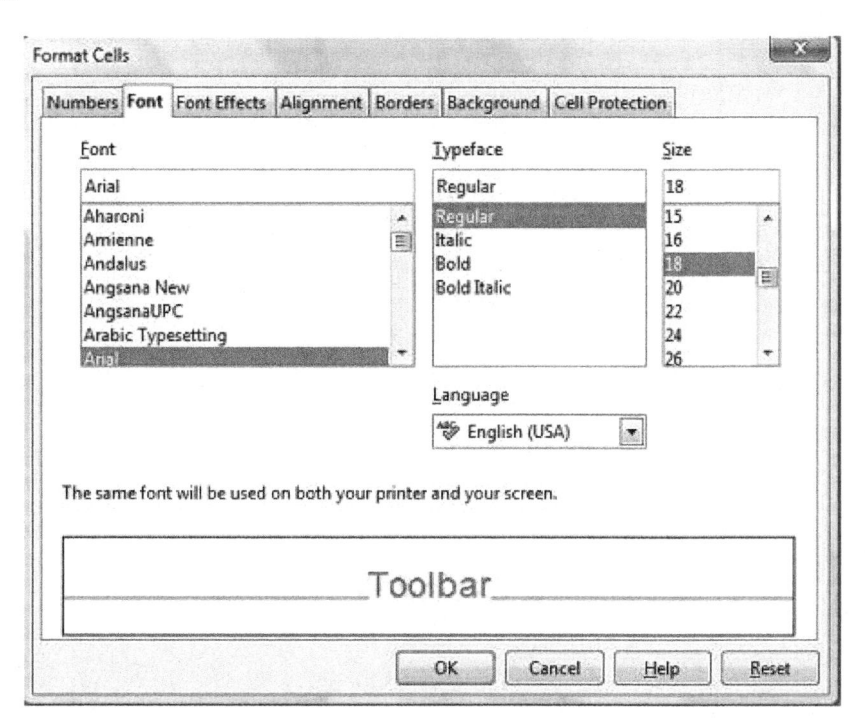

Figure 4

115

Step 4: Click the **Font** tab located at the top of the Format Cells dialog box.

Step 5: From the **Size** scroll list, select the preferred Font Size.

Step 6: Click the **Font Effects** tab located along the top of the Format Cells dialog box.

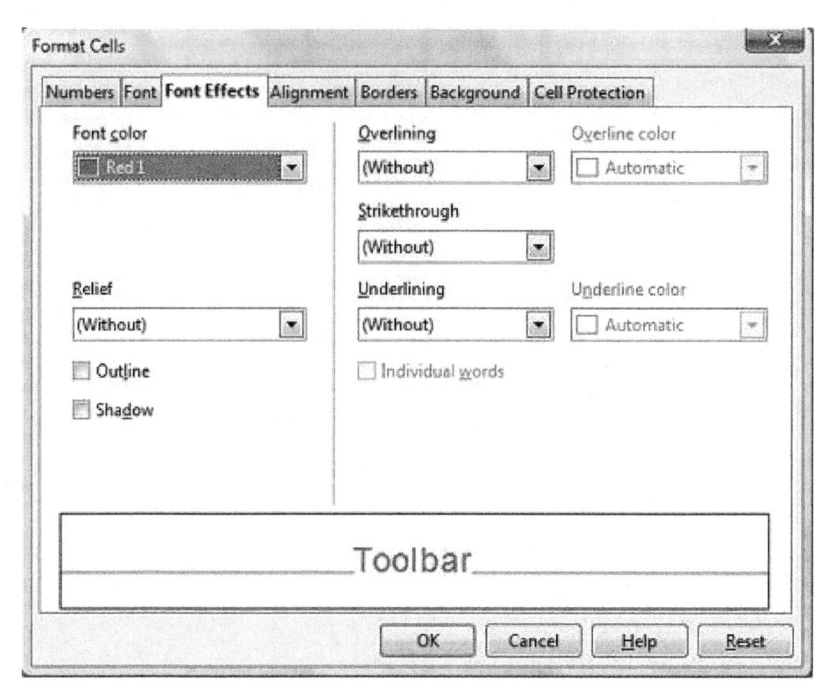

Figure 5

Step 7: In the **Font Color** drop-down menu, select the preferred Font Color.

Step 8: Click **OK**. The specified changes will be applied to the text within the selected cells.

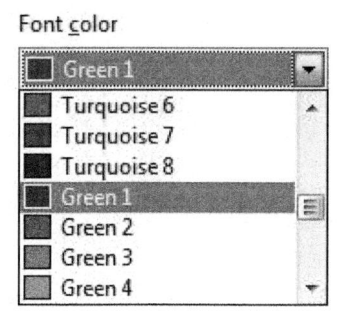

Figure 6

Growth & Assessment

1. What are two ways to change the color, font, and size of text?

2. Which tab do users select from the Format Cells dialog box to modify font color?

3. How do users change the font color using the Toolbar?

Section 3.4 – Using the Borders Button

Section Objective:

- Learn how to use the Borders button.

Adding Cell Borders

OpenOffice Calc allows users to change the border of a single cell or all of the cells within a spreadsheet. This is a helpful feature when trying to draw attention to certain cells within a spreadsheet. The following steps outline how this is done.

Step 1: Create a new Calc spreadsheet. Using the left mouse button, click and drag the cursor over a group of cells. The selected cells will have a boarder applied to them.

Step 2: Locate the Toolbar on the Menu Bar. Click the arrow next to **Border** and select the desired border. Once selected, the boarder will be applied to the previously selected cells.

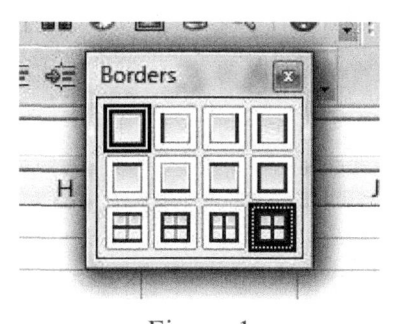

Figure 1

Modifying Cell Borders

OpenOffice Calc allows users to modify the border once it has been applied to the desired cells. A user can alter the color, the line style and the spacing of the cell border. The following steps outline how to access these border options.

Step 1: Click **Format**, located on the Menu Bar.

Step 2: From in the Format drop-down menu, click **Cells…**. The **Format Cells** dialog box will appear.

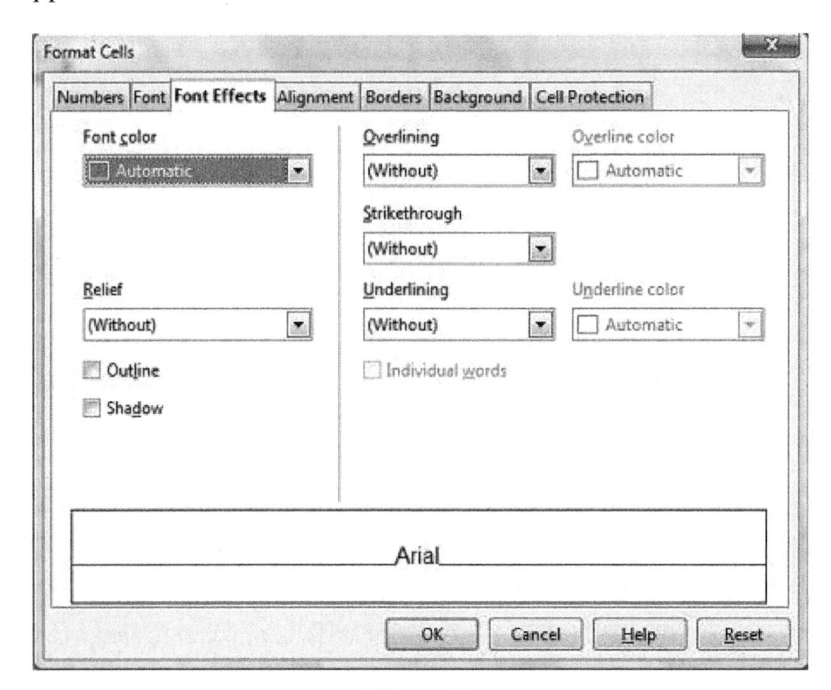

Figure 2

Step 3: Click the **Borders** tab located along the top of the Format Cells dialog box.

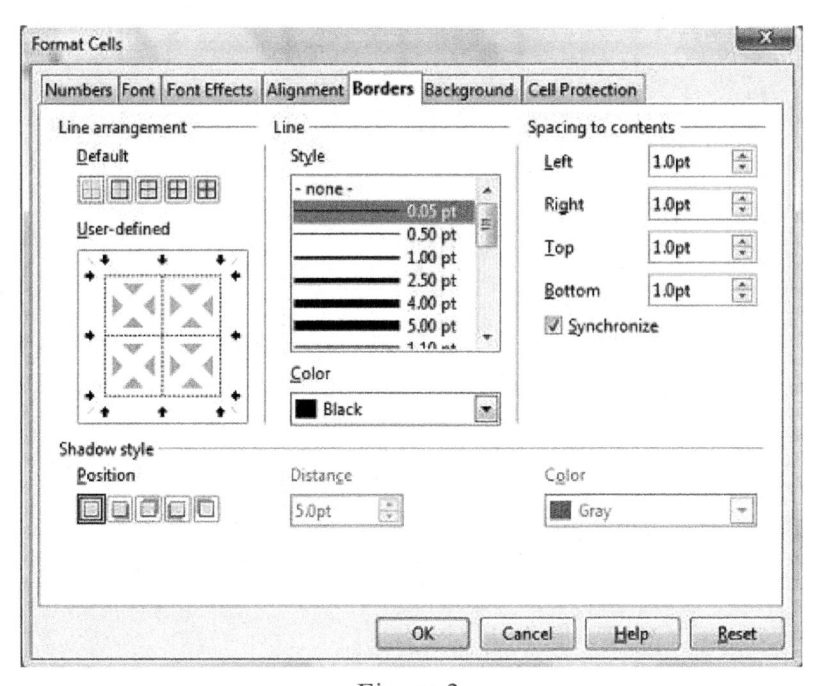

Figure 3

Step 4: Here, select the color, line style and the spacing of the cell border. Once the desired modifications have been made, click **OK**. The new border format will be applied to the selected cells.

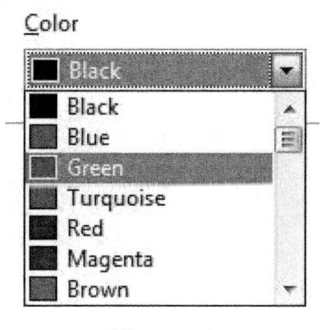

Figure 4

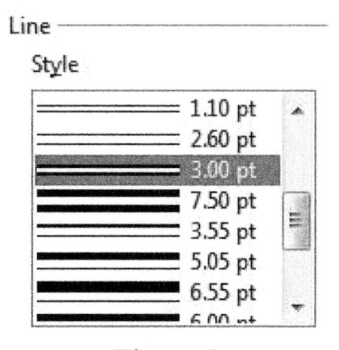

Figure 5

Deleting Cell Borders

The borders added to the selected cells are not permanent; the user has the ability to delete them at any time. The following steps outline how this is done.

Step 1: Using the left mouse button, click and drag the cursor over a group of cells that have a border applied to them.

Step 2: Once the cells have been selected, **right-click** anywhere within the selected cells. From the Quick Menu, select **Default Formatting**. The selected cells will return to the original format.

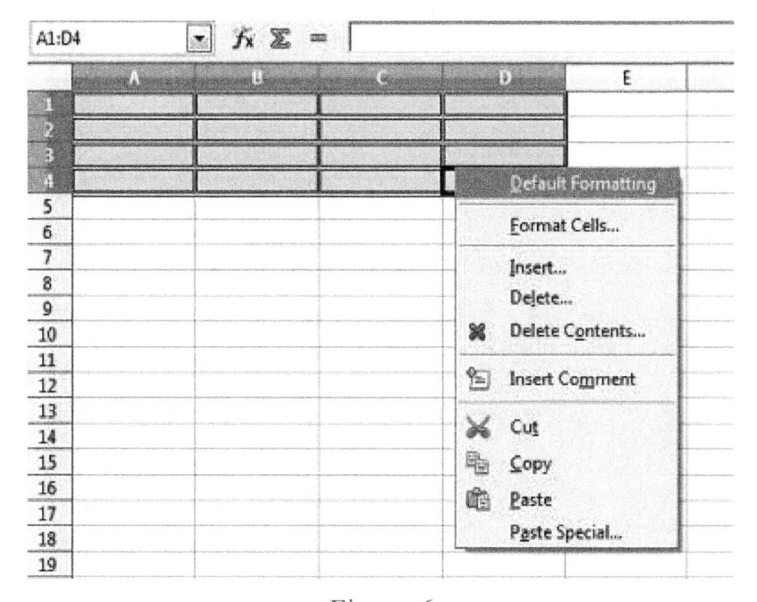

Figure 6

119

Growth & Assessment

1. Calc allows users to change the border of single cells as well as multiple cells within a spreadsheet.

    a. TRUE

    b. FALSE

2. Using the Quick Menu, what option would users select to delete cell borders?

3. Border formatting is only applied to a selected cell's border.

    a. TRUE

    b. FALSE

Section 3.5 – Using the Fill Button

Section Objective:

- Learn how to use the Fill button.

Using the Fill Button

OpenOffice Calc provides multiple ways to repeat information in many cells throughout a spreadsheet. The most convenient way to repeat information in contiguous cells is by using the **Fill** command. The Fill command allows users to easily repeat a cell's contents, regardless of the content's complexity, in additional cells. The following steps outline the various ways this can be done.

Filling Cells Using the Edit Menu

Step 1: Enter data into any cell within the spreadsheet.

Figure 1

Step 2: Starting with the cell containing the data to be copied, select the group of cells to be filled.

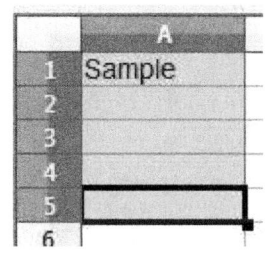

Figure 2

Step 3: Click **Edit**, located on the Menu Bar.

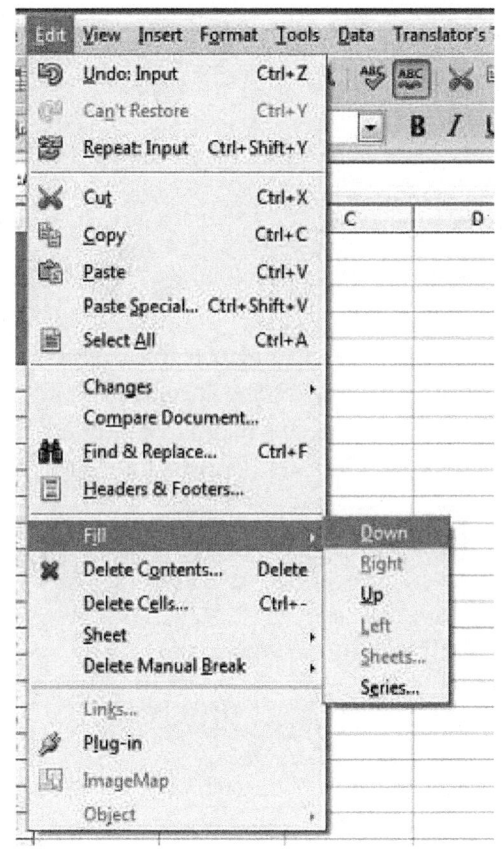

Figure 3

Step 4: From the Edit drop-down menu, click **Fill** and then select the appropriate option based on the cells that will be filled. Once the preferred option has been selected, the cells will be filled.

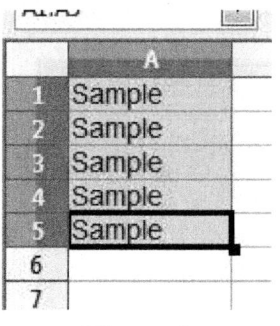

Figure 4

Filling Cells Using the Mouse

In OpenOffice Calc, users can also perform a Fill by using the mouse. This saves the time of having to navigate the Menu Bar. The following steps outline how this is done.

Step 1: Enter data into any cell within the spreadsheet.

Step 2: Enter data either below or to the right of the first cell.

Step 3: Highlight both cells and move the cursor over the fill corner on the second cell so it changes into **crosshairs**.

Figure 5

Step 4: Using the left mouse button, click and hold the **crosshairs**.

Step 5: Drag the crosshairs in the preferred direction. The Fill will be applied to all cells the crosshairs highlight.

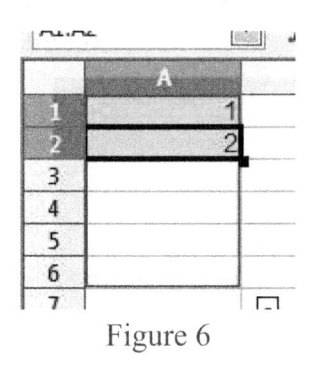

Figure 6

Step 6: Release the left mouse button. The **Fill** will be applied to the selected cells.

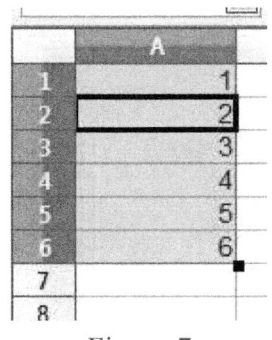

Figure 7

Filling Cells Using the Mouse

123

Growth & Assessment

1. What is the most convenient way to repeat information in many different cells?

2. Where is the Fill command located?

3. Where is the fill corner located?

4. The cursor will change to crosshairs when positioned over the fill corner.

    a. TRUE

    b. FALSE

Section 3.6 – Exporting Spreadsheets to a PDF

Section Objective:

- Learn how to export spreadsheets to a PDF.

Exporting Spreadsheets to a PDF

OpenOffice Calc allows users to export spreadsheets to a PDF file type. PDF stands for **Portable Document Format**. The PDF file is the industry-standard file format for file viewing and file sending. PDF files are sent because others can view the document even if they don't have the proper software to view a Calc spreadsheet.

OpenOffice Calc provides users with two options when exporting a Calc spreadsheet to a PDF. This section covers both options. The first set of steps will outline how users can export directly to a PDF while having Calc make all of the formatting decisions. The second set of steps will also outline how to export a spreadsheet to a PDF, but this option allows users to select the formatting options rather than having the application do it automatically.

Exporting Directly to a PDF

Step 1: Open a previously saved Calc spreadsheet.

Step 2: Click the **Export to PDF** button found on the **Toolbar**. The **Export** dialog box will appear.

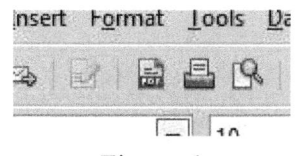

Figure 1

Step 3: The **Export** dialog box will display a screen where the user is able to enter a file name and select the destination folder in which the exported file will be saved. Once the desired information has been entered, click **Save**. The spreadsheet will be exported as a PDF file and stored in the selected folder.

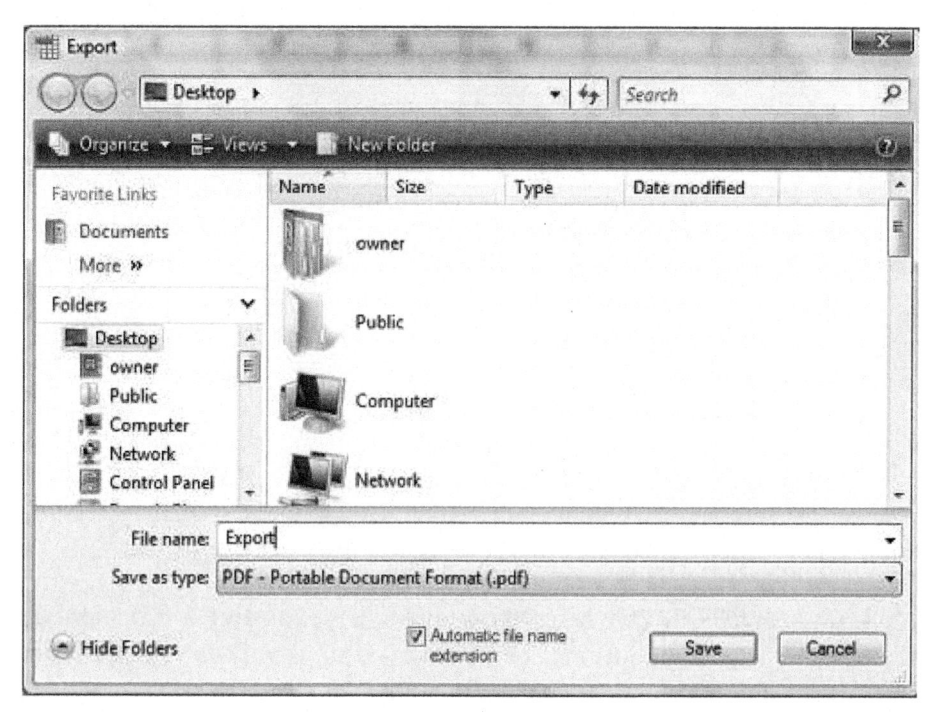

Figure 2

Step 4: Access the folder in which the PDF was saved. Once the folder has been opened, double-click on the PDF file icon and the PDF file will open.

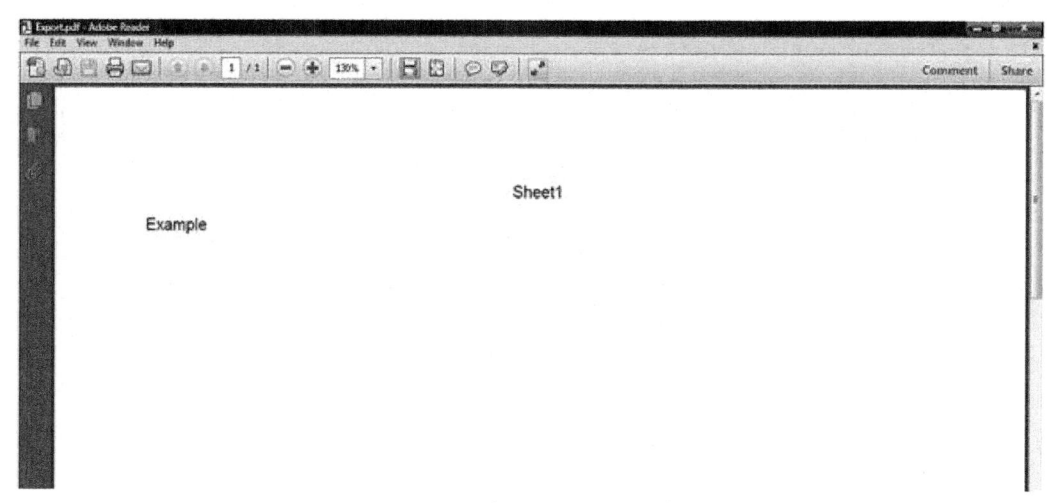

Figure 3

Exporting through the PDF Options Dialog Box

Exporting a spreadsheet through the **PDF Options** dialog box allows users to modify the specifics of the exported file. The following steps will provide users with information on the different modifications that can be made in the **PDF Options** dialog box, and will also outline how this task is done.

Step 1: Open a previously saved Calc spreadsheet.

Step 2: Click **File**, located on the Menu Bar.

Step 3: From the File drop-down menu, select **Export as PDF…**. The **PDF Options** dialog box will appear with the **General** tab selected.

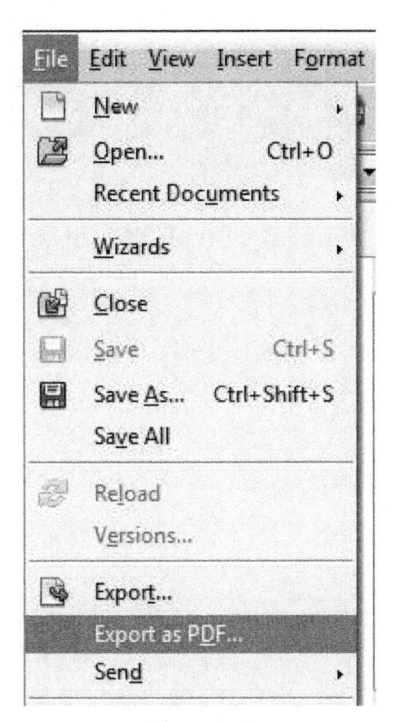

Figure 4

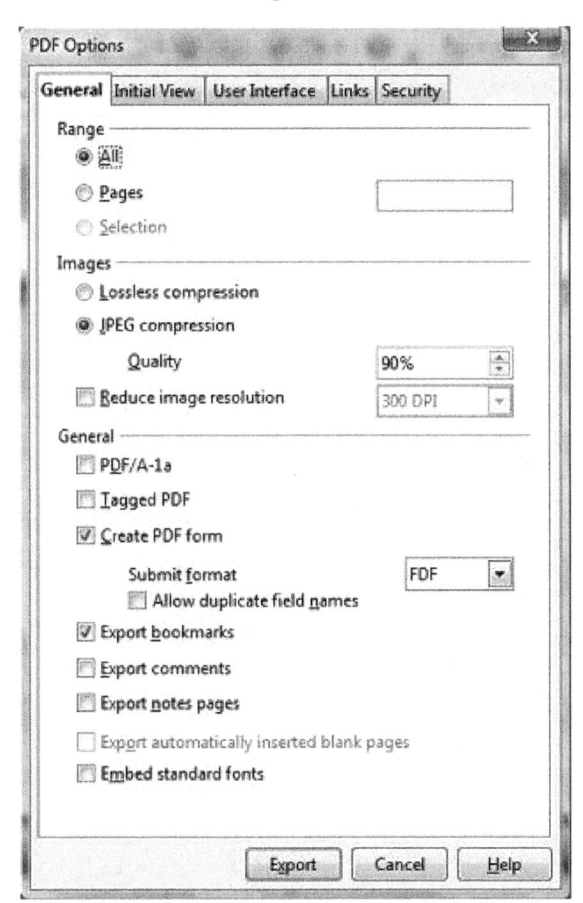

Figure 5

127

Step 4: Within the **General** tab, users can choose which pages to include in the PDF, the type of compression to use for images (this will affect the size and the quality of the images), as well as other options. Select the desired options.

Step 5: Click the **Initial View** tab. Within this tab, users have the ability to choose how the PDF opens by default in the PDF reader. This will be used to open the exported spreadsheet. Select the desired options.

Note – Many options will be left at their default value.

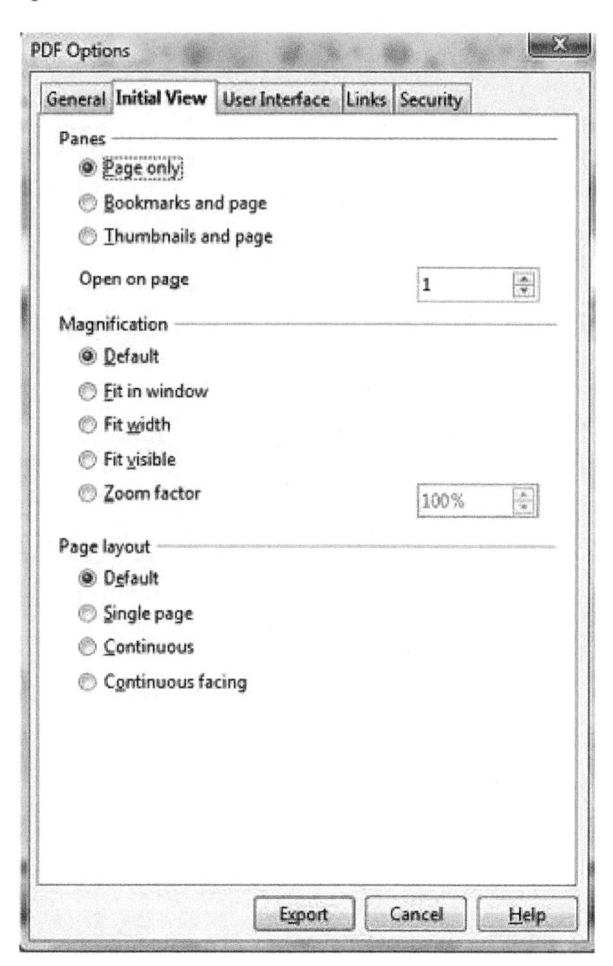

Figure 6

Step 6: Click the **User Interface** tab. Within this tab, users have the ability to modify more settings to control how a PDF reader displays the exported spreadsheet. Select the desired modifications.

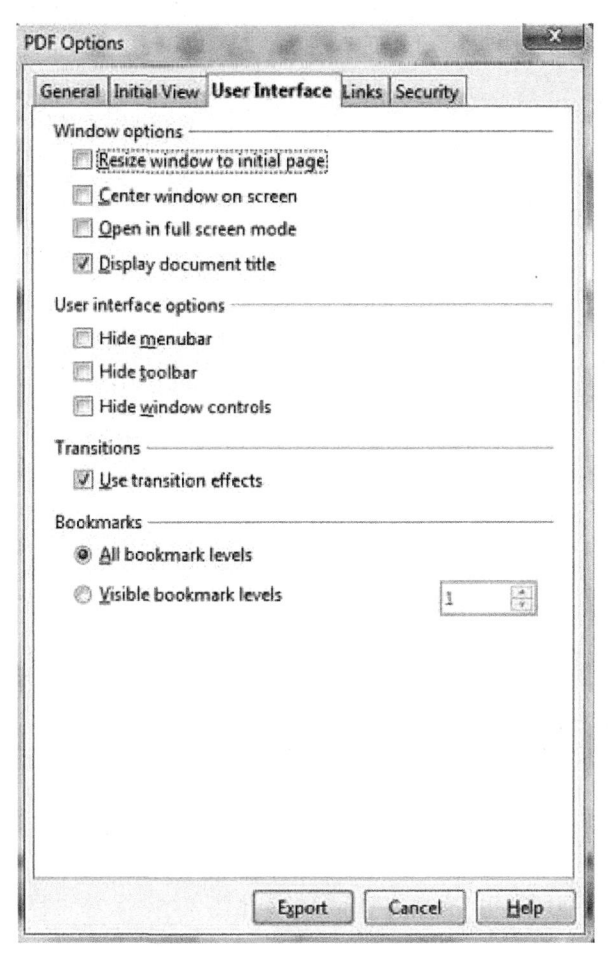

Figure 7

Step 7: Click the **Links** tab. Within this tab, users can choose how to manage any links between the exported PDF file and the original Calc spreadsheet file.

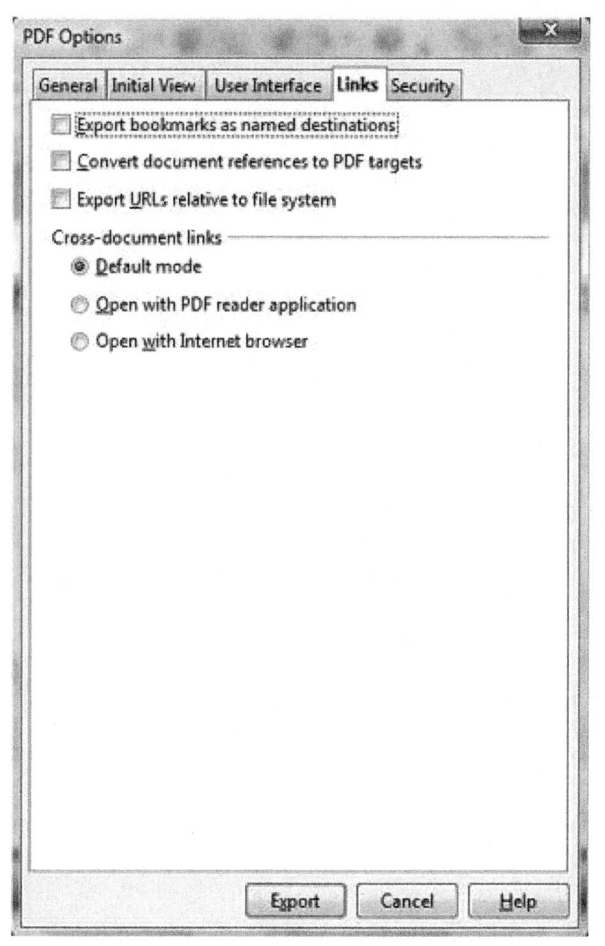

Figure 8

Step 8: Click the **Security** tab. Within this tab, users have the ability to make the exported PDF password protected. If a password is desired, the pane will offer additional fields that protect the document from being altered.

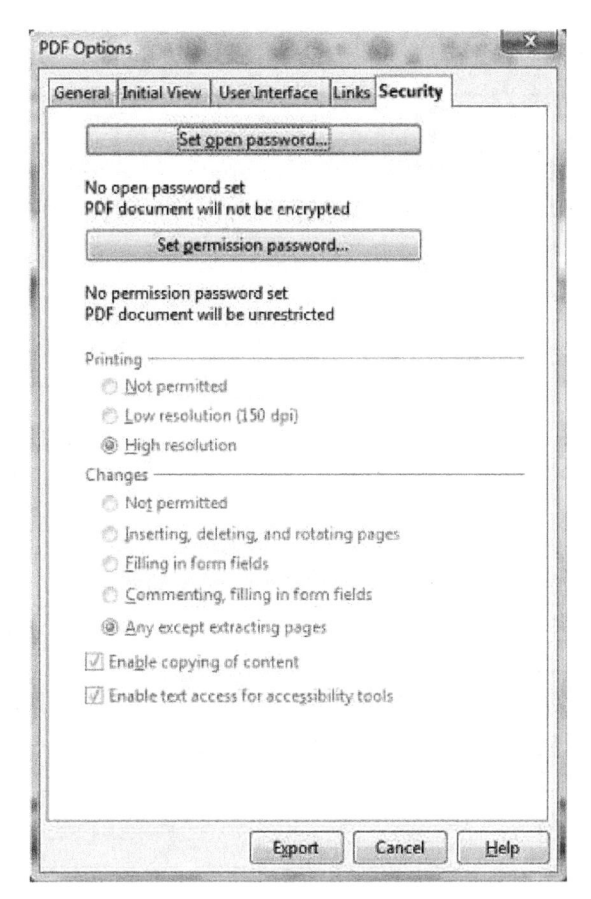

Figure 9

Step 9: Click the **Export** button at the bottom of the dialog box. The **Export** dialog box will appear.

Step 10: The **Export** dialog box will display a screen where the user is able to enter a file name and select the destination folder in which the exported file will be saved. Once the desired information has been entered, click **Save**. The spreadsheet will be exported as a PDF file and stored in the selected folder.

Growth & Assessment

1. What does PDF stand for?

2. What important option is found within the Security tab?

3. The PDF file is the industry-standard file format for file viewing and file sending.

    a. TRUE

    b. FALSE

4. What kinds of options are found within the General tab?

Section 3.7 – Applying Formatting to Numbers

Section Objective:

- Learn how to apply formatting to numbers.

Formatting Numbers in Calc

OpenOffice Calc allows users to not only format the text but also format numerical values. Users can apply various formatting options to numerical values through the **Format Cells** dialog box. The following steps outline how this is done.

Step 1: Create a new Calc spreadsheet and enter a number into any cell. Once a number has been entered into a cell, select the cell.

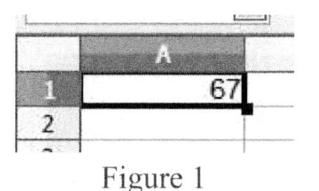

Figure 1

Step 2: Click **Format**, located on the Menu Bar.

Step 3: From the Format drop-down menu, click **Cells…**. The **Format Cells** dialog box will appear with the **Numbers** tab selected.

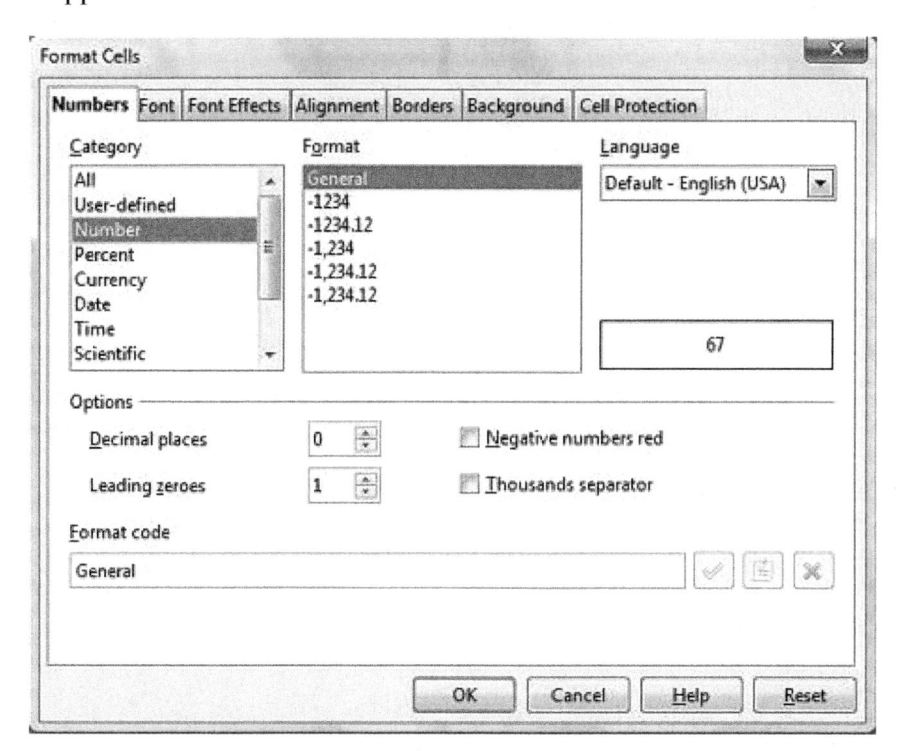

Figure 2

Step 4: From the **Category** list, select the preferred number type. The number types available include User-define, Number, Percent, Currency, Date, Time, Scientific, Fraction, Boolean Value, and Text.

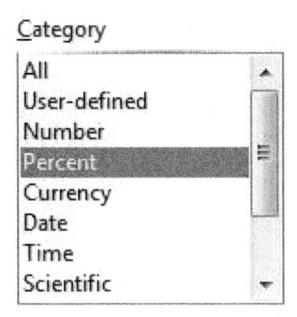

Figure 3

Step 5: From the **Format** list, users can choose the formatting used for the selected category. Select the desired format for the Category type selected in Step 4.

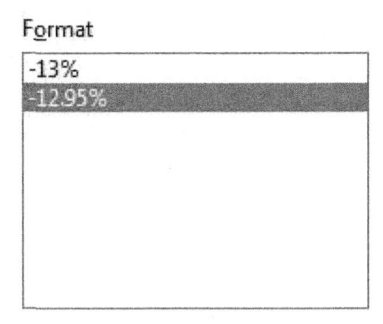

Figure 4

Step 6: From the **Options** portion of the Numbers tab, users have the ability to manually format what the number will look like when displayed in the spreadsheet. The variables that Calc will allow the users to adjust will depend on the Category type selected in Step 4.

Decimal places – This option controls how many decimal places, to the right of the decimal, will be displayed. For instance, if "3" was selected using the arrows, a possible outcome would be "12.126."

Leading zeroes – This option determines how many zeroes will be displayed to the left of the decimal point. For instance, if "3" was selected using the arrows, a possible outcome would be "000.1."

Figure 5

Step 7: Click **OK**. The selected cell will be formatted as specified in the **Format Cell** dialog box.

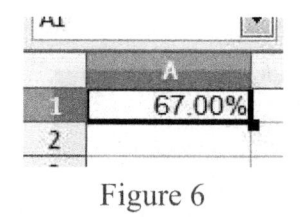

Figure 6

Note – Calc also allows users to change the format of numbers through the Toolbar. The Toolbar provides buttons which change the selected numbers to Currency, Percentages, and Standard. The Toolbar also allows users to modify the number of decimal places used for the number.

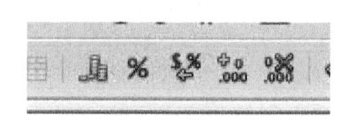

Figure 7

Growth & Assessment

1. Calc allows users to format numbers.

    a. TRUE

    b. FALSE

2. What two options are offered under the **Options** portion of the Numbers tab?

3. List three of the options under **Category**.

Section 3.8 – Adding Date and Time

Section Objective:

- Learn how to add dynamic and static dates and times.

Adding Dynamic and Static Dates and Times

OpenOffice Calc provides users with two options when adding the date and time to a spreadsheet. By default, **Dynamic** dates and times are updated every time Calc is refreshed. This is useful if the user wants the current date and/or time to be displayed every time the spreadsheet is viewed or printed. **Static** dates and times will not be updated like dynamic dates and times. Once the date/or time is entered into the spreadsheet, it will not change unless the user manually changes it. This is useful when a user is collecting data over a period of time and the date and/or time in which the data was collected is important. The following steps cover both of these options.

Steps for Adding a Dynamic Date and Time:

Step 1: Select a cell in which the date will appear.

Step 2: In the cell, type '=**today()**.'

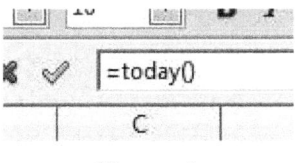

Figure 1

Step 3: Press **ENTER**. The current date will appear in the selected cell and will be updated every time the Calc spreadsheet refreshes. To insert the current time, type '=**now()**' into the cell and press **ENTER**. The current time will appear.

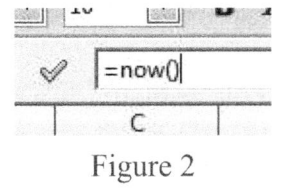

Figure 2

Steps for Adding a Dynamic Date and Time:

As stated above, a **Static** date and/or time will not be updated like a dynamic date and/or time. The following steps outline how this option is applied to a spreadsheet.

Applying a Static Date

Step 1: Select a cell in which the date will appear.

Step 2: In the cell, type '=**date()**.'

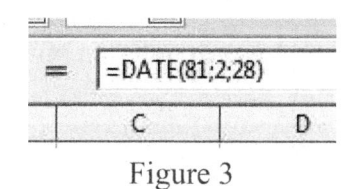

Figure 3

Step 3: Press **ENTER**. The current date will appear in the selected cell and will stay the same regardless of other actions taken in the application.

Applying a Static Time

Step 1: Select a cell in which the time will appear.

Step 2: In the cell, type '=**time0**.'

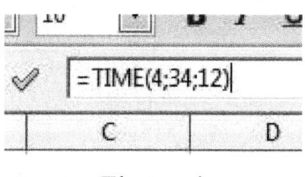

Figure 4

Step 3: Press **ENTER**. The current time will appear in the selected cell and will stay the same regardless of other actions taken in the application.

Growth & Assessment

1. What command is used to display the current time?

2. What command is used to display the current date?

3. The command '=time0' is used to apply a static date.

    a. TRUE

    b. FALSE

4. What happens when a static date is applied to a particular cell?

Section 3.9 – Using Headers and Footers

Section Objective:

- Learn how to add Headers and Footers.

Adding Headers and Footers in Calc

OpenOffice Calc allows users to add Headers and Footers to spreadsheets. Headers and Footers are useful tools when organizing a spreadsheet. A Header is a section of information that is displayed above the cells in a spreadsheet, and a Footer is a section of information displayed below the cells in a spreadsheet. Information that is typically included within the Header and/or Footer is the user's name, the document's name, page numbers, and the date and/or time. Though this is the typical information entered into these portions of the spreadsheet, users can include any information desired. The following steps outline how to add a Header and Footer to a spreadsheet.

Step 1: Create a new Calc spreadsheet.

Step 2: Click **Format**, located on the Menu Bar.

Step 3: From the Format drop-down menu, click **Page…**. The **Page Style: Default** dialog box will appear.

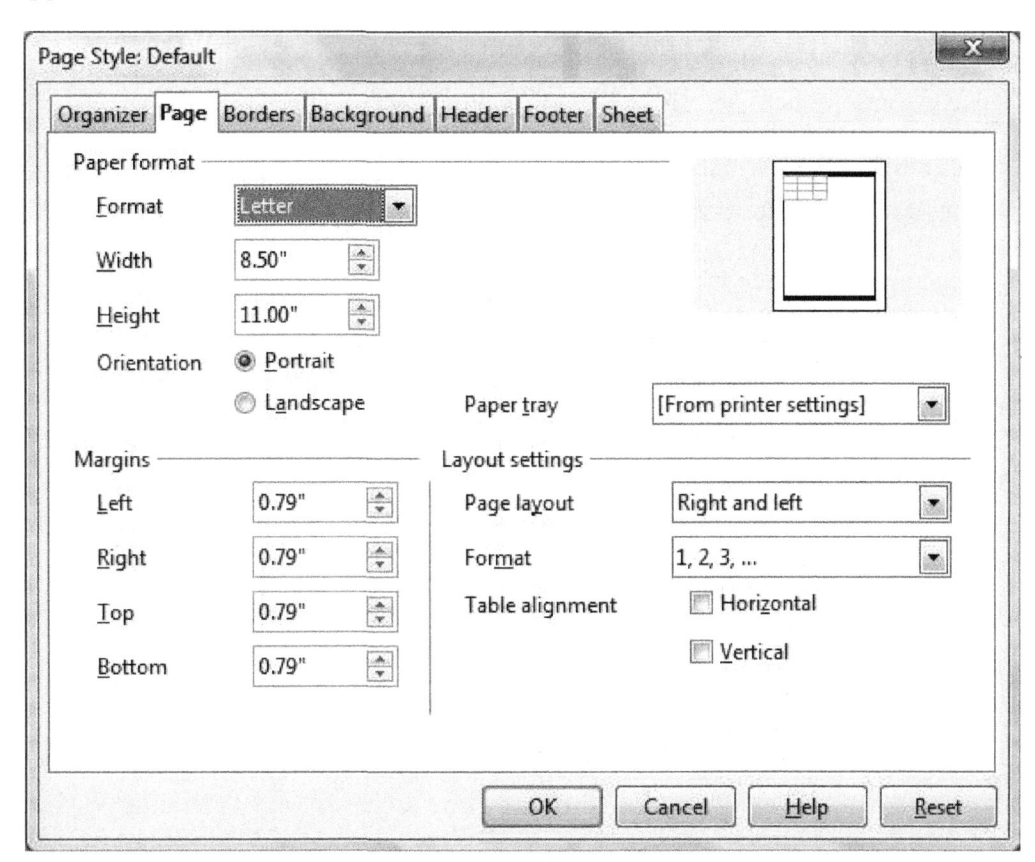

Figure 1

Step 4: Select the **Header** tab. Here, the available Header options are displayed.

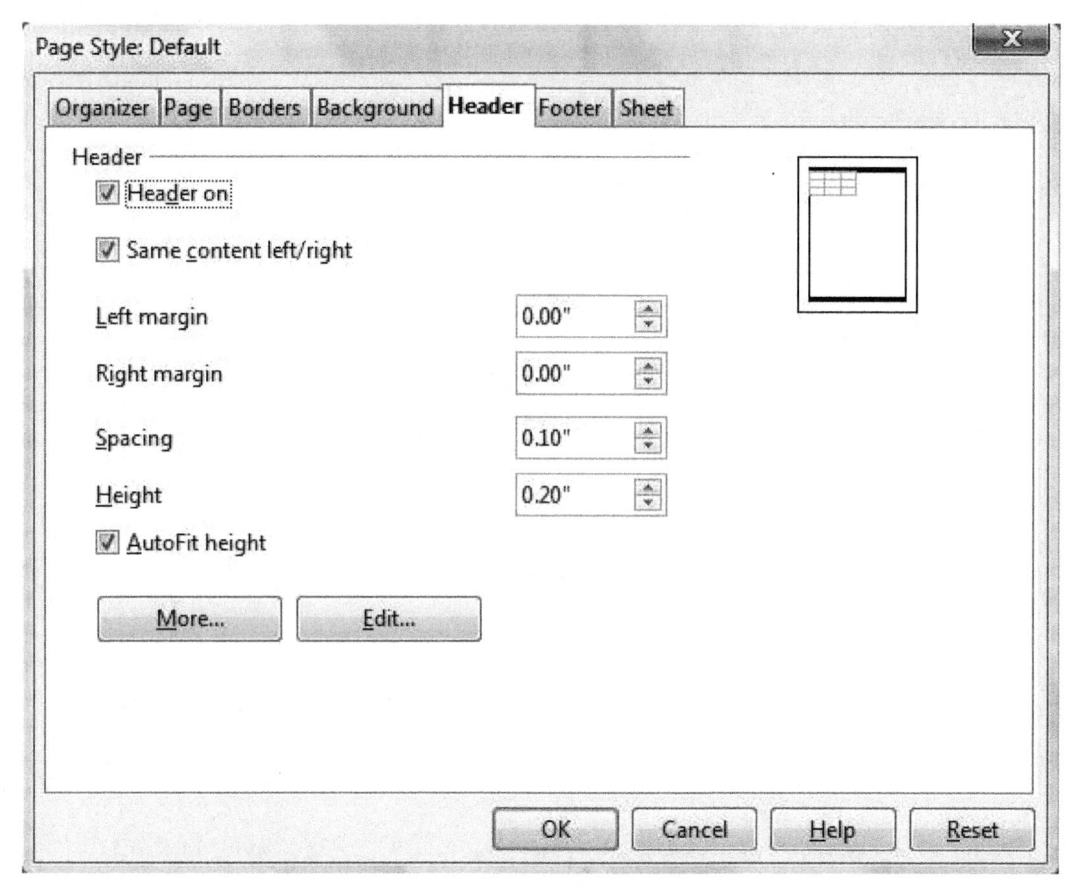

Figure 2

Note – To access the **Footer** options, select the **Footer** tab located next to the Header tab in the Page Style: Default dialog box.

Step 5: Within the Header dialog box, users have the ability to modify various elements of the header. The options available in the Header dialog box are listed below.

- Whether or not the Header is included in printouts
- The margins of the Header in respect to the edges of the page
- The spacing between lines of text in the Header
- The height of the Header
- Whether or not Calc should automatically adjust the height of the header

Step 6: Once the desired header options have been specified, click the **Edit...** button. The **Header (Page Style: Default)** dialog box will appear. Here, users can edit the contents of the Header.

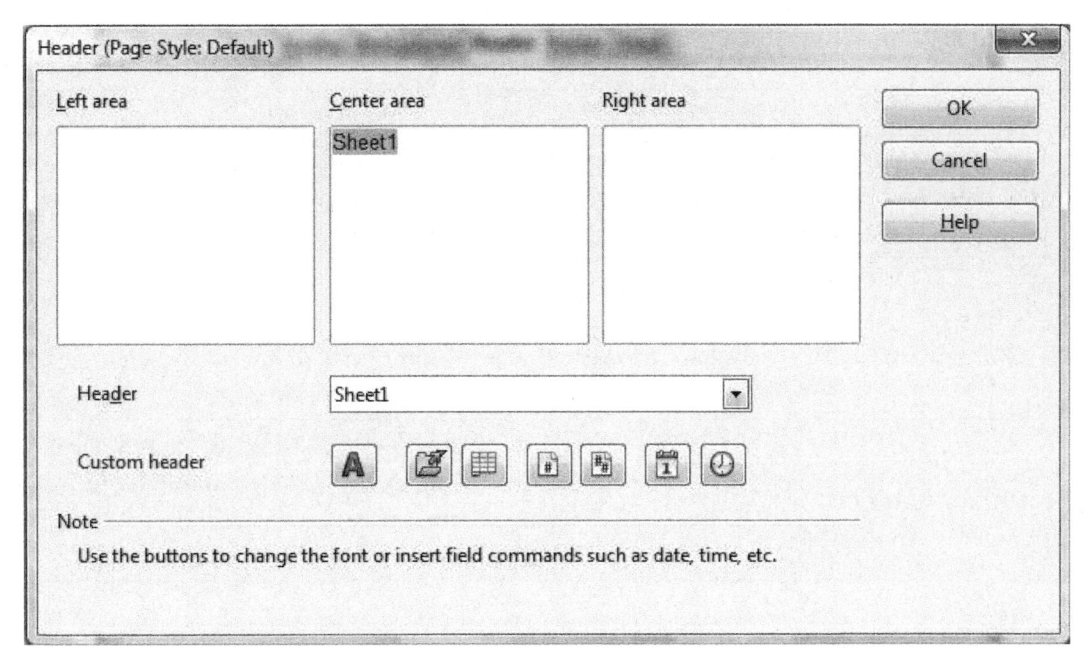

Figure 3

Step 7: In the **Left Section**, **Center Section**, and **Right Section** textboxes, enter the desired information which will be displayed in the Header or Footer.

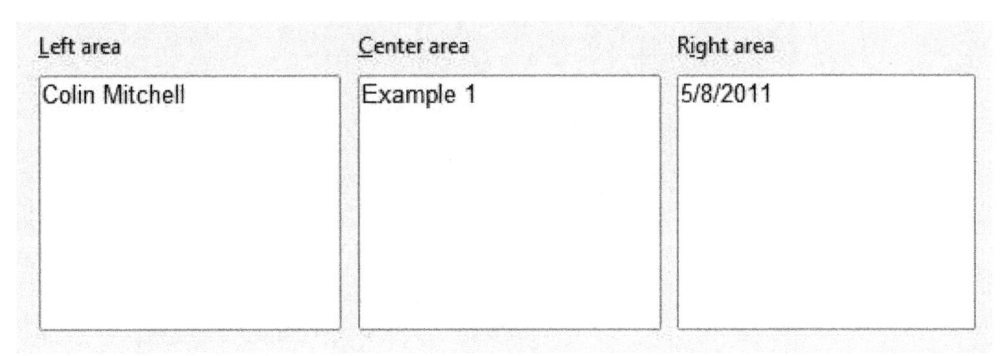

Figure 4

Step 8: Calc provides a series of buttons that the user can click to modify the Header and/or Footer. Clicking these buttons will insert the corresponding information into the region where the cursor is, within the Header or Footer.

Figure 5

The table below describes the action each button performs.

Name	Icon	Action
Font Controls		Opens up the Font dialog box. From here the user can change the formatting of characters used in the Header/Footer.
File Name place holder		Inserts a place holder for the file name of the spreadsheet. For example if the name of the spreadsheet file is "Example", then this is what will be inserted into the Header/Footer.
Sheet Place holder		Inserts a place holder for the sheet name of the spreadsheet. For example if the name of the sheet is "Sheet 1", then this is what will be inserted into the Header/Footer.
Page Number Place Holder		Inserts the page number into the Header/Footer.
Total Pages Place Holder		Inserts the total pages into the Header/Footer.
Date Place Holder		Adds a Date place holder to the Header/Footer. It will update automatically to the current date when the spreadsheet is refreshed or saved.
Time Place Holder		Adds a Time place holder to the Header/Footer. It will update automatically to the current time when the spreadsheet is refreshed or saved.

Step 9: When finished, click **OK**. The **Header (Page Style: Default)** dialog box will close.

Step 10: Click **OK**. The **Page Setup** dialog box will close.

Growth & Assessment

1. Where is a Header located?

2. A Footer is located at the top of a spreadsheet.

    a. TRUE

    b. FALSE

3. What does the Date Place Holder do?

4. What is the purpose of Font Controls?

Section 3.10 – Formatting Cells Using Conditional Formatting

Section Objective:

- Learn how to format cells using Conditional Formatting.

Conditional Formatting

OpenOffice Calc allows users to format specific cells using Conditional Formatting. Conditional Formatting allows users to only apply a particular format to cells which satisfy a certain set of criteria. The criteria can be number-based (e.g., greater than, less than, equal to), text-based (e.g., text contains, date occurring), or both (e.g., duplicate values).

This section will explain how to format specific cells within a spreadsheet using Conditional Formatting. Before following the steps provided in this section, create a new Calc spreadsheet and enter the same data as shown in the figure below.

	A	B	C	D	E
1	First Name	Last Name	District	# of Clients	Sales Amount
2	John	Davies	Philadelphia	9	$1,235,241.00
3	Ken	Paul	Philadelphia	7	$1,234,234.00
4	Amy	Hoch	Pittsburgh	16	$8,342,412.00
5	Chris	Mitchell	Pittsburgh	12	$12,312,312.00
6	Josh	Flaim	Pittsburgh	14	$7,463,134.00
7	John	Riggins	Los Angeles	11	$5,832,953.00
8	Amy	Krallinger	Los Angeles	6	$981,573.00
9					

Figure 1

Note – Multiple formatting options are available when using Conditional Formatting; however, this section explains how to format specific cells for educational purposes.

Step 1: Select the range of cells to be formatted.

	E
	Sales Amount
9	$1,235,241.00
7	$1,234,234.00
16	$8,342,412.00
12	$12,312,312.00
14	$7,463,134.00
11	$5,832,953.00
6	$981,573.00

Figure 2

Step 2: Click **Format**, located on the Menu Bar.

Step 3: From the Format drop-down menu, select **Conditional Formatting…**. The **Conditional Formatting** dialog box will appear.

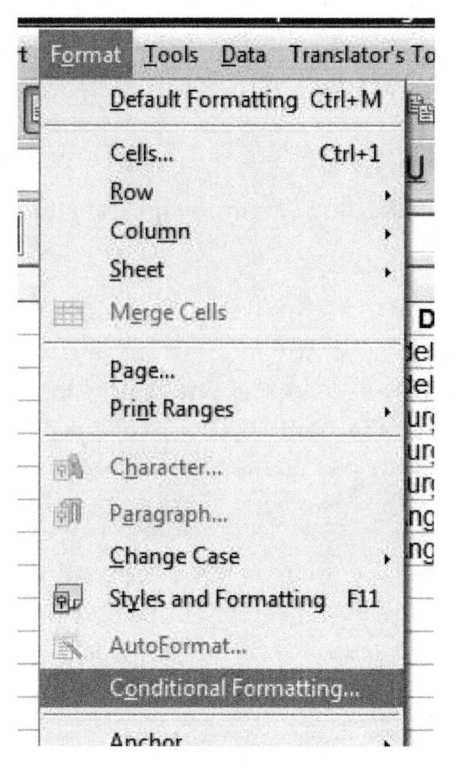

Figure 3

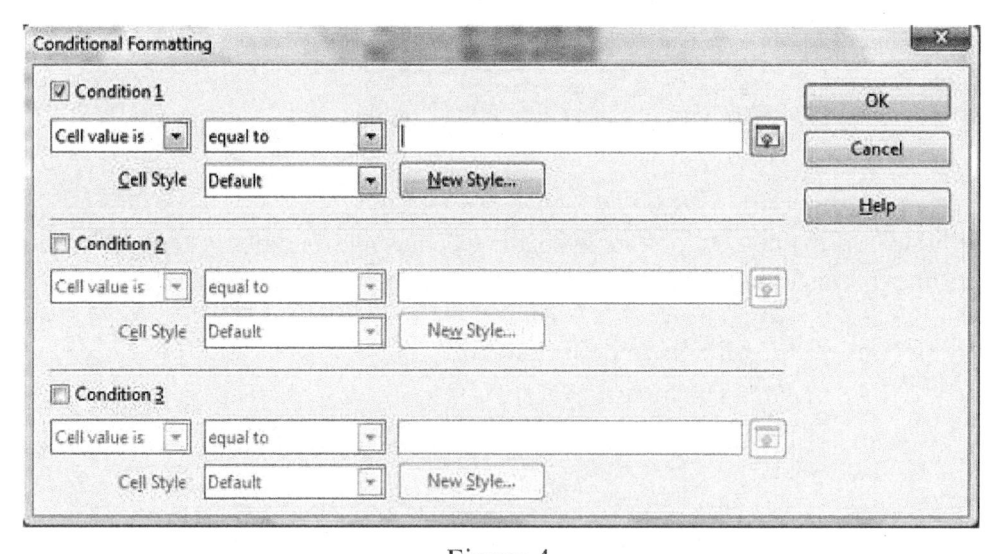

Figure 4

Step 4: The **Condition 1** checkbox will be checked, allowing the user to make modifications.

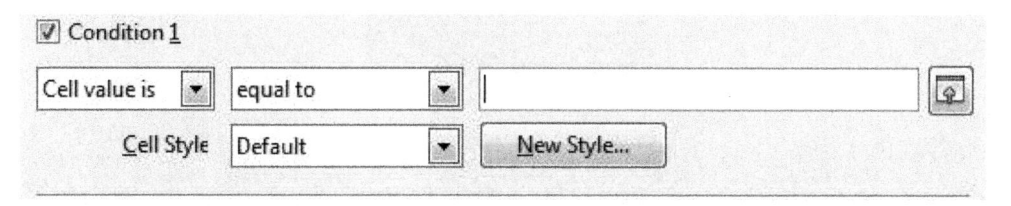

Figure 5

Step 5: The drop-down menu, located on the left-hand side of the dialog box, allows users to choose whether the condition will be based on the contents of the cell, or a formula that is present in the cell. For this example, keep the value in the drop-down as **Cell value is**.

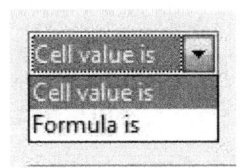

Figure 6

Step 6: Moving to the right within the dialog box, the next drop-down menu will contain the actual conditional operator that will be used to set the desired formatting. For this example, select the **less than** operator.

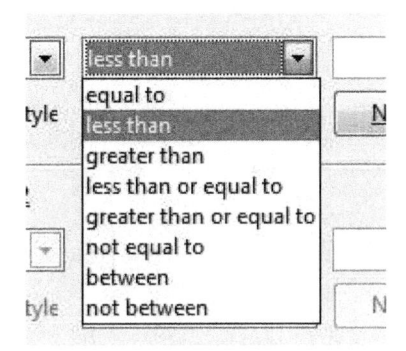

Figure 7

Step 7: The next textbox is where the user will enter the value that the application uses to determine whether the conditional formatting will be applied to a particular cell. Users have the ability to either manually enter the value into the textbox, or click on the **Shrink** button to select the cell(s) that contains the value needed. For this example, enter the number "**5000000**" into the **Value** textbox.

Figure 8

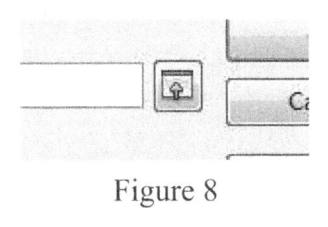

Figure 9

Step 8: The final drop-down menu, located on the right-hand side of the dialog box, is where users have the ability to select the **Cell Style** which will be applied to a cell if it meets the specified conditions. This drop-down menu will include all of the styles available in Calc, as well as any styles the user has previously created. For this example, select **Result**.

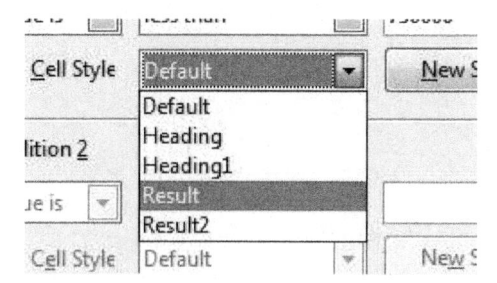

Figure 10

Step 9: Once the various options have been selected, click **Ok**. The conditional formatting is applied to any cells that satisfy the specified criteria.

Figure 11

Note – More than one conditional formatting rule can be selected. This is done by clicking the checkbox next to **Condition 2**, **Condition 3**, **etc…**, and then following the steps provided above.

Growth & Assessment

1. Conditional Formatting allows the user to only apply a particular format to cells which satisfy a certain set of criteria.

    a. TRUE

    b. FALSE

2. What options are located in the final drop-down menu?

3. More than one conditional formatting rule can be selected.

    a. TRUE

    b. FALSE

Section 3.11 – Creating a Customized Conditional Formatting Style

Section Objective:

- Learn how to create a customized Conditional Formatting style.

Customized Conditional Format Style

OpenOffice Calc allows users to create a customized Conditional Formatting style by accessing the New Formatting Rule dialog box. This is useful when the preformatted rules, such as highlighting, are not desired. This section will outline how users can do this and apply the customized formatting style to the spreadsheet.

Note – To better explain the process of creating a customized Conditional Formatting style, the following steps require the user to create a new Calc spreadsheet and enter the data found in the figure below:

	A	B	C	D	E
1	First Name	Last Name	District	# of Clients	Sales Amount
2	John	Davies	Philadelphia	9	$1,235,241.00
3	Ken	Paul	Philadelphia	7	$1,234,234.00
4	Amy	Hoch	Pittsburgh	16	$8,342,412.00
5	Chris	Mitchell	Pittsburgh	12	$12,312,312.00
6	Josh	Flaim	Pittsburgh	14	$7,463,134.00
7	John	Riggins	Los Angeles	11	$5,832,953.00
8	Amy	Krallinger	Los Angeles	6	$981,573.00
9					

Figure 1

Step 1: Select the range of cells to be formatted.

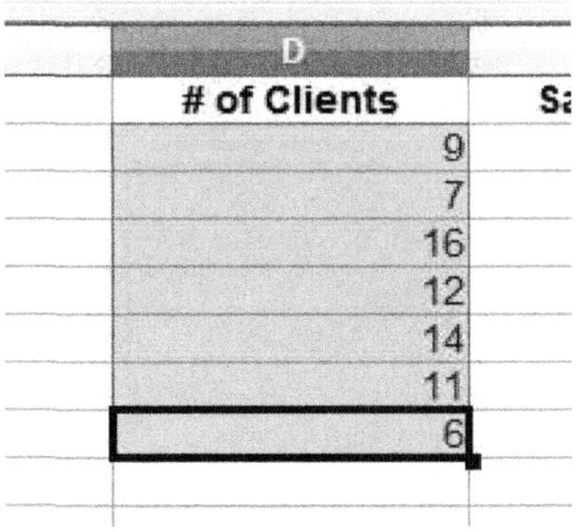

Figure 2

Step 2: Click **Format**, located on the Menu Bar.

145

Step 3: From in the Format drop-down menu, click **Conditional Formatting…**. The **Conditional Formatting** dialog box will appear.

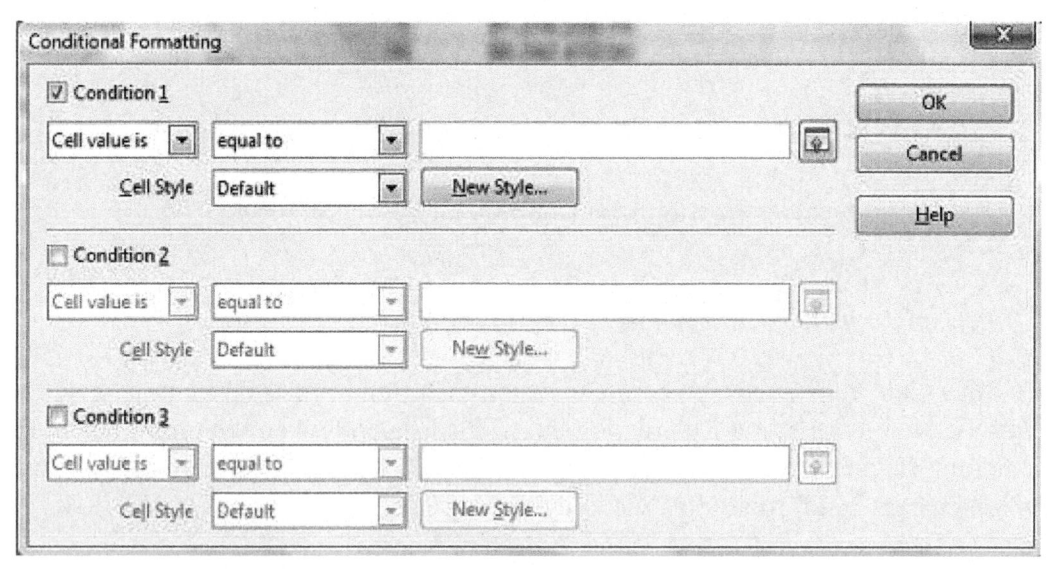

Figure 3

Step 4: Fill in the drop-down menus as displayed in the figure below:

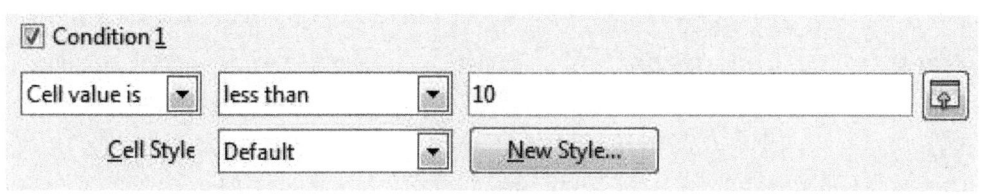

Figure 4

Step 5: Click the **New Style…** button. The **Cell Style** dialog box will appear with the **Organizer** tab displayed.

Figure 5

Steps 6: Within this tab, users have the ability to enter the name for the new style. For this example, enter "**Lesson 11 Style**."

Step 7: Click the **Numbers** tab. Here, users can select how the numbers will be displayed within the cells once the formatting has been completed. For this example, select the formatting as shown in the figure below.

Note – If the style will not be used for cells containing numbers, the user can skip the **Numbers** tab.

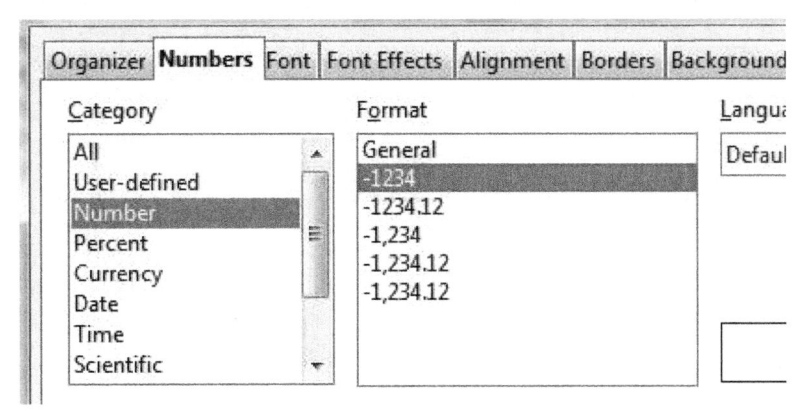

Figure 6

Step 8: Click the **Font** and **Font Effect** tabs to modify how the text will be displayed within the cells. For this example, refer to the figure below to identify the necessary selections.

Figure 7

Step 9: Click the **Alignment** tab. The Alignment tab allows users to choose where the data will be located within the cell. For this example, set up the alignment as shown below.

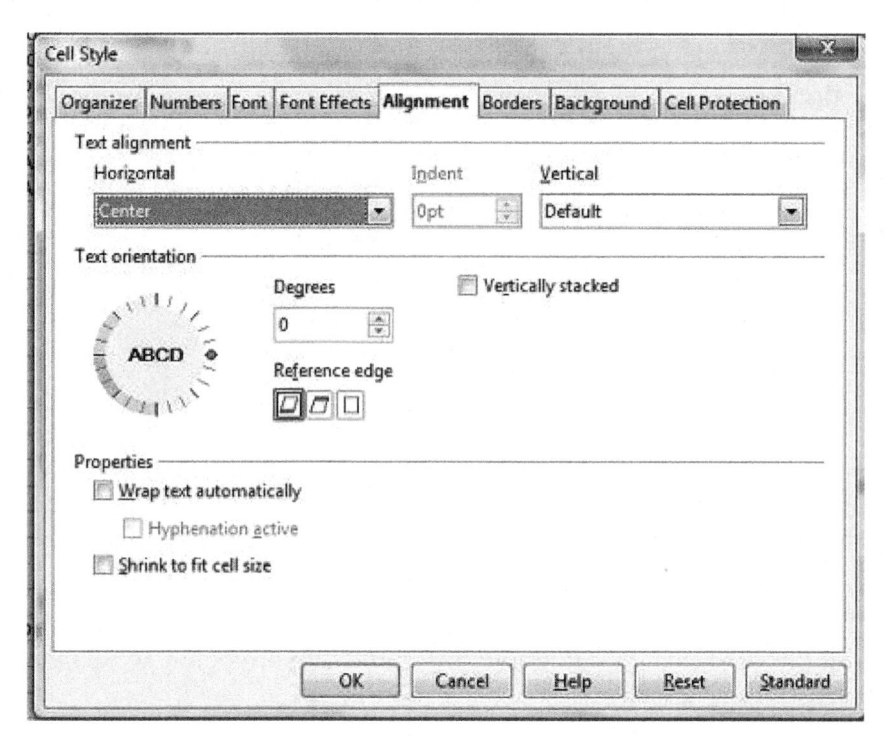

Figure 8

Step 10: Click the **Border** tab. The Border tab allows users to design borders for the cells that meet the specified criteria. Select the preferred style and width of the border.

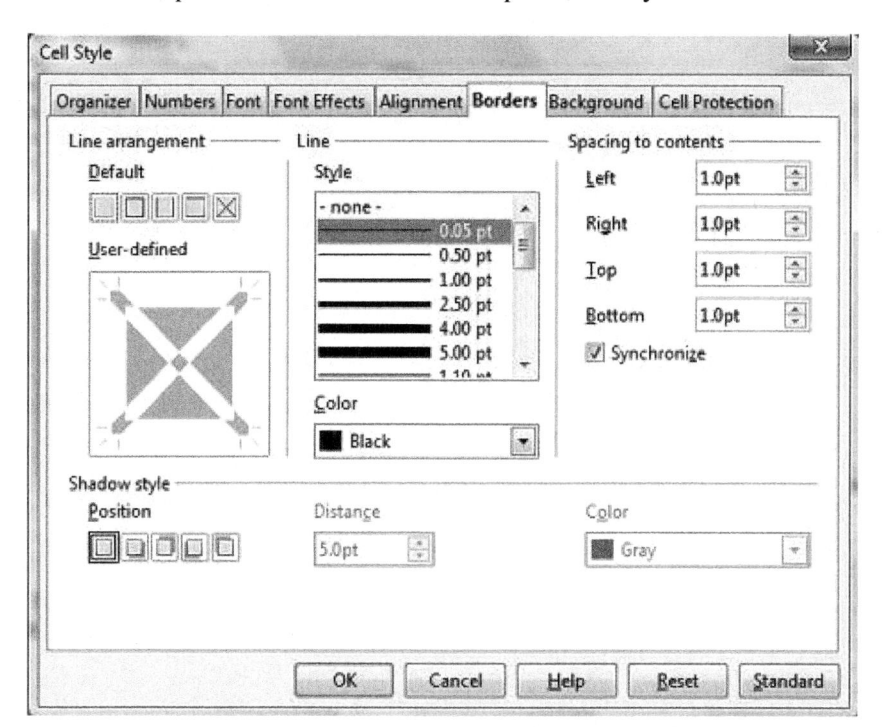

Figure 9

Step 11: Click the **Background** tab. The Background tab allows users to select a background color for the cells that meet the specified criteria. For this example, set the background color to **Red**.

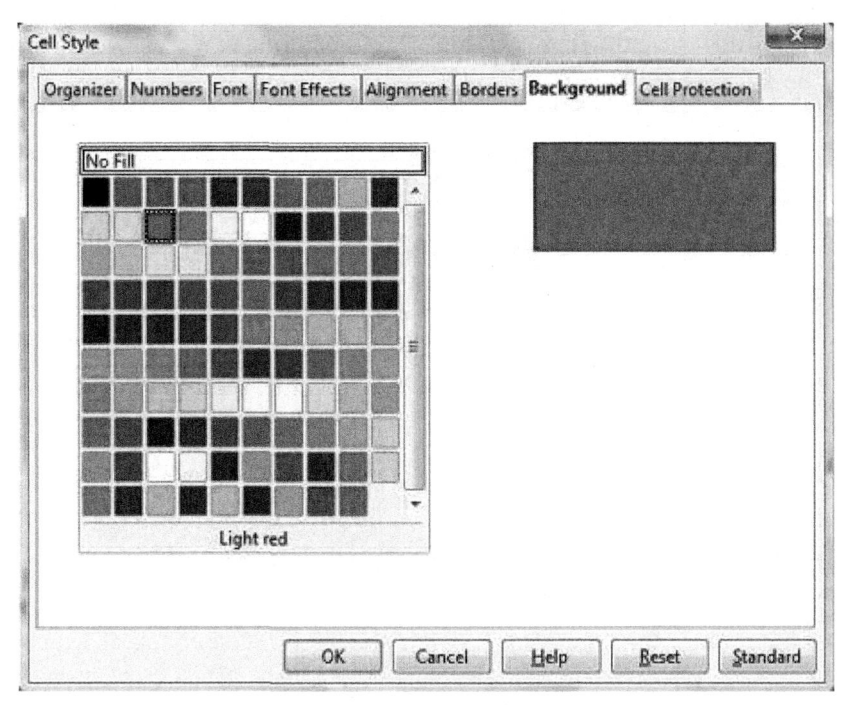

Figure 10

Step 12: Click the **Cell Protection** tab. The Cell Protection tab allows users to hide any cells that meet the specified criteria. Users can also choose to hide the cells only when printing. Since this example is meant to teach users how to create a conditional formatting style, no changes within this tab are necessary.

Figure 11

Step 13: Click **OK**. The created style will automatically be the chosen style in the **Cell Style** drop-down menu.

Step 14: Once verifying that the recently created style is selected, click **OK** on the **Conditional Formatting** window. The customized conditional formatting style will be applied to the selected cells.

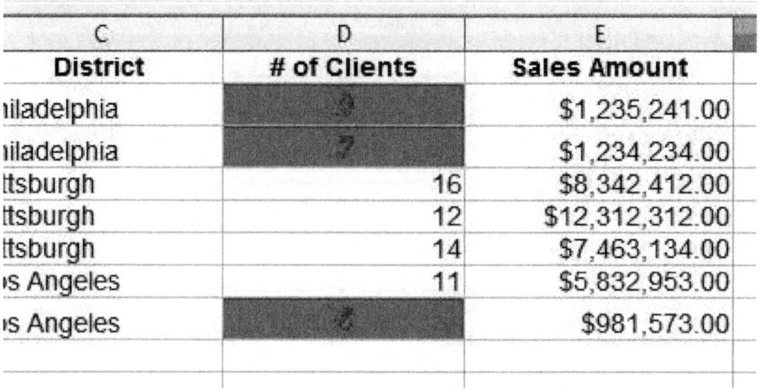

District	# of Clients	Sales Amount
iladelphia		$1,235,241.00
iladelphia		$1,234,234.00
ttsburgh	16	$8,342,412.00
ttsburgh	12	$12,312,312.00
ttsburgh	14	$7,463,134.00
s Angeles	11	$5,832,953.00
s Angeles		$981,573.00

Figure 16

Growth & Assessment

1. OpenOffice Calc allows users to create a customized Conditional Formatting style.

    a. TRUE

    b. FALSE

2. What does the Alignment tab allow users to do?

3. What is the purpose of the background tab?

Section 3.12 – Editing Conditional Formatting Styles

Section Objectives:

- Learn how to edit Conditional Formatting styles.

Edit Conditional Formatting Styles

In OpenOffice Calc, the conditional formatting styles can be modified if needed. Calc allows users to modify customized styles, as well as the application's preformatted styles. The following steps outline how to modify both types of styles used for conditional formatting.

Step 1: Create a new Calc spreadsheet.

Step 2: Click **Format**, located on the Menu Bar.

Step 3: From the Format drop-down menu, select **Styles and Formatting**. The **Styles and Formatting** dialog box will appear.

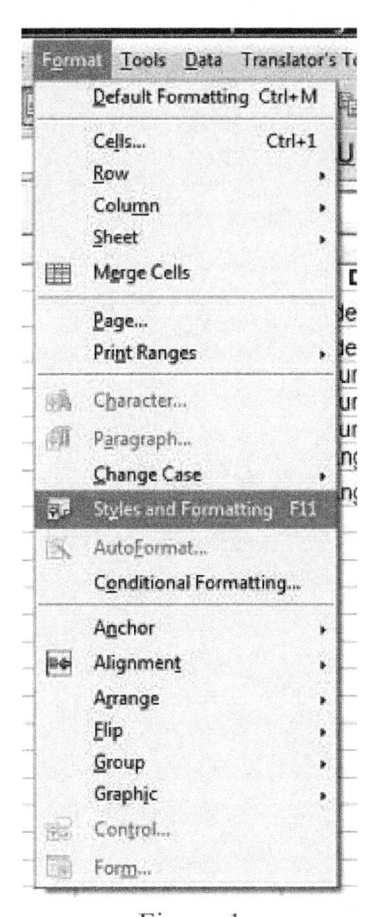

Figure 1

151

Step 4: Select any of the styles found within the **Styles and Formatting** dialog box. Users have the ability to modify both types of styles (customized and preformatted). Once the style, that is to be modified, has been selected, **right-click** on the style. The Quick Menu will appear.

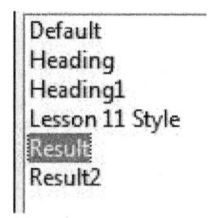

Figure 2

Step 5: From the **Quick Menu**, select **Modify…**. The **Cell Style** dialog box will appear.

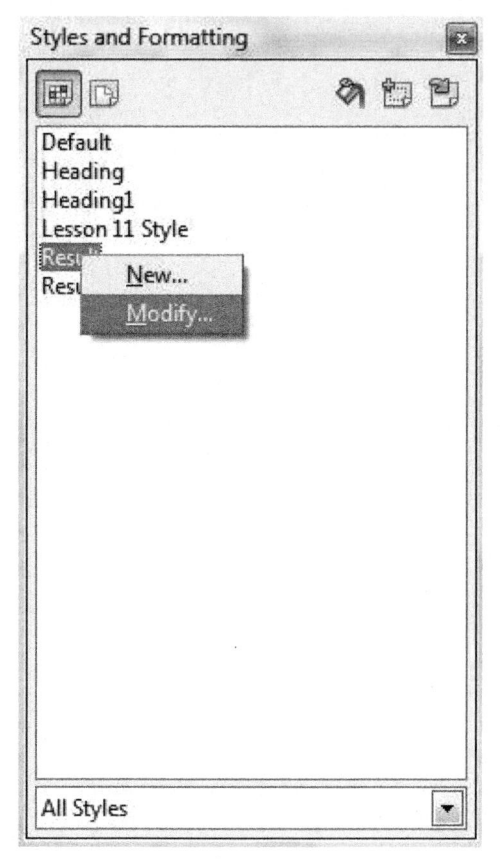

Figure 3

152

Step 6: Within the Cell Style dialog box, select the different tabs to view the various options. Make the preferred modifications to the Conditional Formatting style and then click **OK** to save the changes.

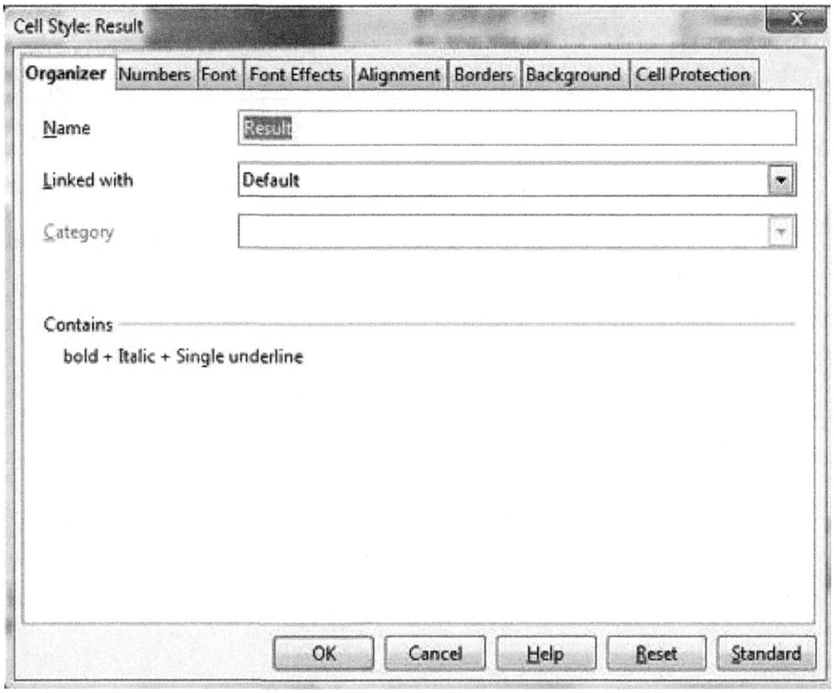

Figure 4

Tabs within the Cell Style: Dialog Box

- Organizer
- Numbers
- Font
- Font Effects
- Alignment
- Borders
- Background
- Cell Protection

Note – If the modified style is currently being use within the spreadsheet, all modifications will be instantly implemented after closing the **Cell Style** dialog box.

Growth & Assessment

1. Calc allows users to edit existing styles.

    a. TRUE

    b. FALSE

2. Where would a user find the different options for conditional formatting?

3. The Styles and Formatting dialog box is used for Conditional Formatting.

    a. TRUE

    b. FALSE

4. List two tabs from the Cell Style dialog box.

Section 3.13 – Positioning Data on a Printout

Section Objective:

- Learn how to position data on a printout.

Selecting the Orientation

In OpenOffice Calc, most documents are portrait (tall) oriented, but many spreadsheets may be easier to read with a landscape (wide) orientation. Calc allows users to select the preferred orientation which is useful when trying to print a large spreadsheet onto one sheet of paper. The following steps outline how to adjust the orientation when printing a spreadsheet.

Step 1: Click **Format**, located on the Menu Bar.

Step 2: From the Format drop-down menu, select **Page…**. The **Page Style: Default** dialog box will appear with the **Page** tab displayed.

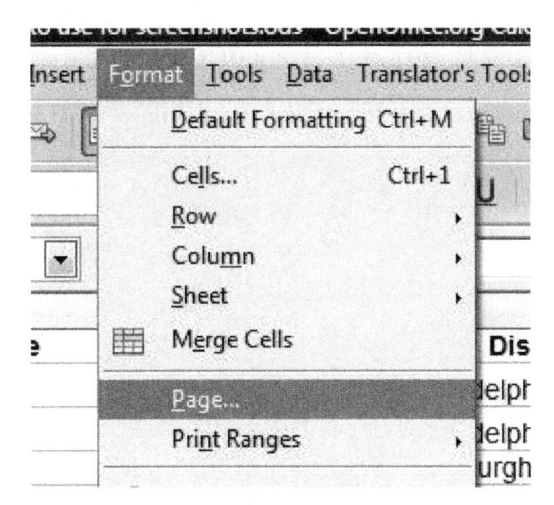

Figure 1

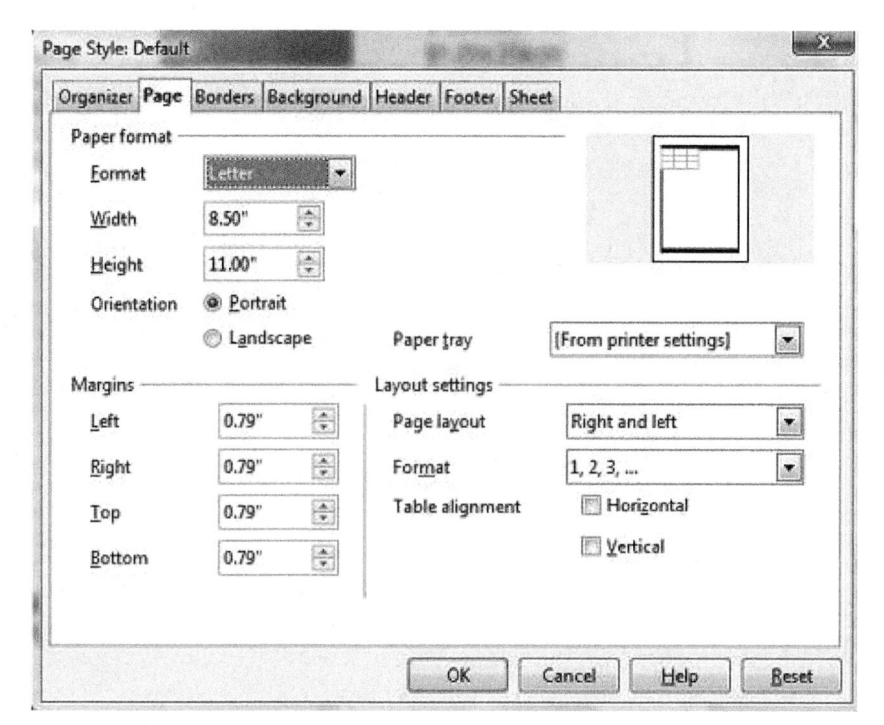

Figure 2

Step 3: Within the **Paper Format** portion of the **Page Style: Default** dialog box, click the radio button next to the preferred orientation. Once the orientation has been identified, click **OK**.

Figure 3

Selecting the Paper Size

When working in Calc, a user's spreadsheet might be so large that it requires different sized printing paper in order to display the data properly. If this is the case, OpenOffice Calc allows users to orient the document to print on a different size paper. The following steps outline how this is done.

Note – The default paper size for OpenOffice Calc is 8 1/2" × 11".

Step 1: Click **Format**, located on the Menu Bar.

Step 2: From the Format drop-down menu, select **Page…**. The **Page Style: Default** dialog box will appear with the **Page** tab displayed.

Step 3: Within the **Paper Format** portion of the **Page Style: Default** dialog box, click on the **Format** drop-down menu to view the different paper measurements available. Once a preferred paper size is selected, the **Width** and **Height** fields will update automatically.

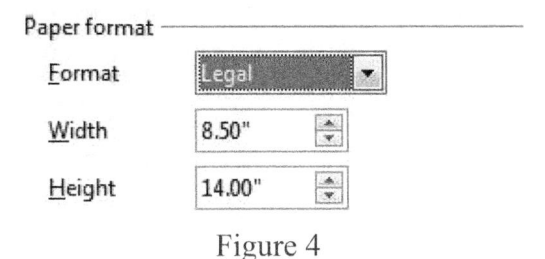

Figure 4

Scaling the Spreadsheet

The scaling option in OpenOffice Calc allows users to adjust the size of the printout. The default size of a printed copy is 100%. The user can adjust the scale to a percentage of the default size, or choose to fit the spreadsheet on a specific number of pages; both options allow the user to reduce or enlarge the entire spreadsheet. Both of these options are outlined below.

Step 1: Select **Format**, located on the Menu Bar.

Step 2: From the Format drop-down menu, select **Page…**. The **Page Style: Default** dialog box will appear with the **Sheet** tab displayed.

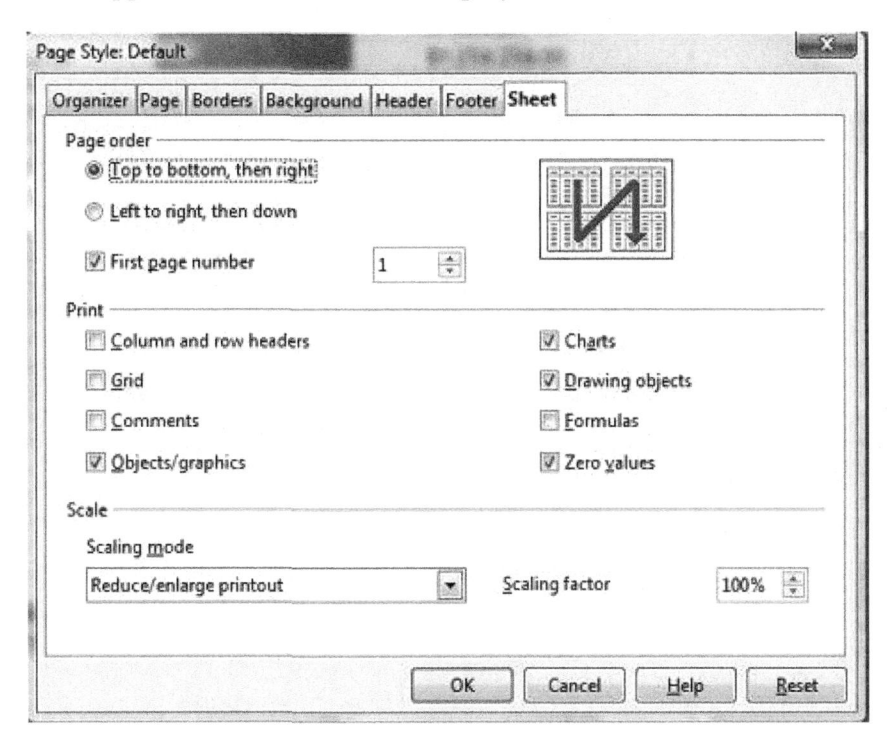

Figure 5

157

Step 3: Within the **Sheet** tab, make sure the **Scaling Mode** drop-down menu is set to **Reduce/Enlarge Printout**. Once verifying that the Reduce/Enlarge Printout option is selected, manually type the desired scaling percentage into the **Scaling factor** textbox.

Note – The Nudge Buttons can also be used to select the appropriate scaling percentage.

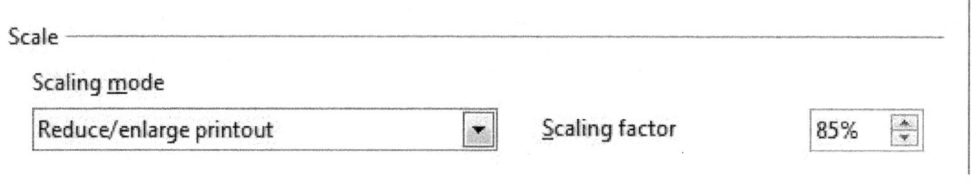

Figure 6

Selecting the Number of Printed Pages

OpenOffice Calc allows users to set a maximum number of pages for a spreadsheet. In order to make the spreadsheet fit within the specified number of pages, the user may choose to re-scale the spreadsheet horizontally, vertically, or both (horizontally and vertically). The following steps outline how this is done.

Step 1: Select **Format**, located on the Menu Bar.

Step 2: From the Format drop-down menu, select **Page…**. The **Page Style: Default** dialog box will appear with the **Sheet** tab displayed.

Step 3: Within the **Sheet** tab, make sure the **Scaling Mode** drop-down menu is set to **Fit print range(s) to width/height**.

Step 4: To re-scale the spreadsheet horizontally within a page limit, perform one of the following actions within the **Scale** portion of the dialog box:

- In the **Width** textbox, enter the appropriate number of pages.

- Click the arrow next to the **Width** textbox and select the desired number of pages.

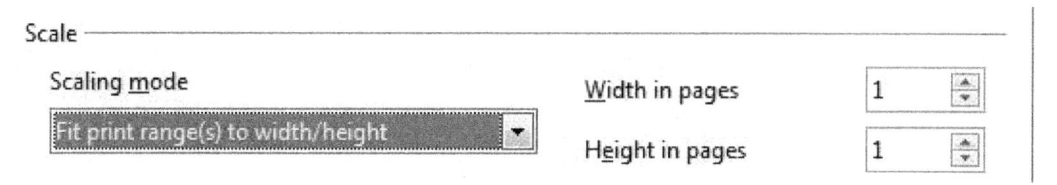

Figure 7

Step 5: To re-scale the spreadsheet vertically within a page limit, perform one of the following actions within the **Scale** portion of the dialog box:

- In the **Height** textbox, enter the appropriate number of pages.

- Click the arrow next to the **Height** textbox and select the desired number of pages.

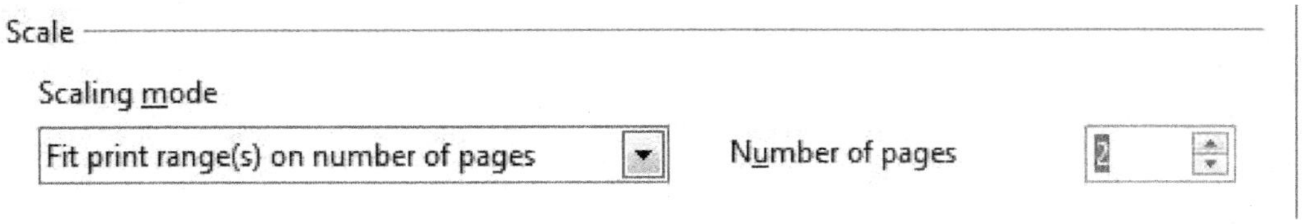

Figure 8

Growth & Assessment

1. Which orientation is considered "tall"?

2. The Nudge Buttons can also be used to select the appropriate scaling percentage.

    a. TRUE

    b. FALSE

3. Which orientation is considered "wide"?

4. What is the height of the default paper size in Calc?

Section 3.14 – Defining Print Area

Section Objective:

- Learn how to define the print area.

Defining the Print Area

OpenOffice Calc, by default, prints all data on a spreadsheet; however, users can define a specific print area from the **Edit Print Ranges** dialog box or by using the **Print Ranges** option located on the Format drop-down menu. The following steps will cover both of these options.

Steps for Using the Edit Print Ranges Dialog Box:

Step 1: Create a new Calc spreadsheet.

Step 2: Click **Format**, located on the Menu Bar.

Step 3: From in the Format drop-down menu, select **Print Ranges** and then **Edit…**. The **Edit Print Ranges** dialog box will appear.

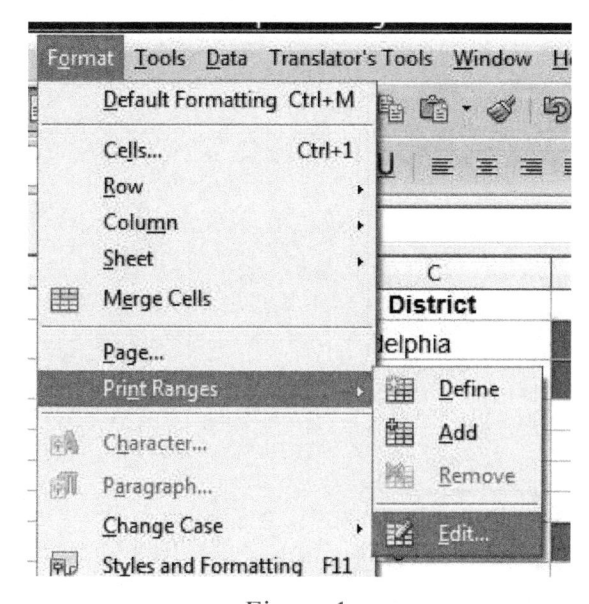

Figure 1

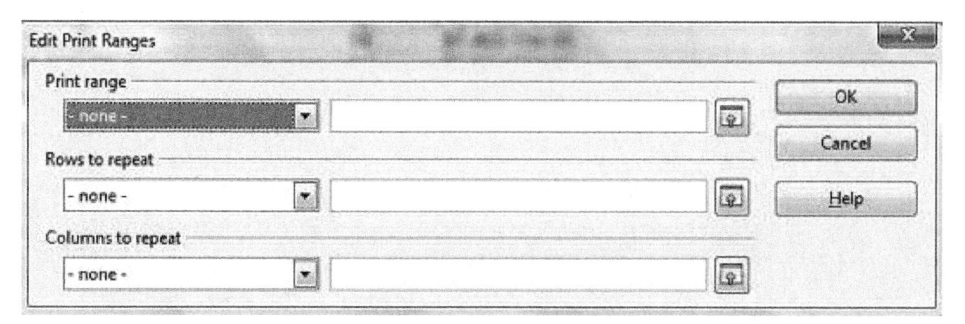

Figure 2

160

Step 4: Within the **Print Range** portion of the dialog box, click the **Shrink** button.

Figure 3

Step 5: Once the dialog box has shrunk, highlight the cells that will be included in the print range. Once highlighted, the cell range will appear in the textbox.

Figure 4

Step 6: Click the **Shrink** button again to return to the dialog box. After verifying that the cell range is correct, click **OK**. The defined print range will be outlined in the spreadsheet.

Note – Calc will keep the selected print area until it is cleared or replaced. To clear the print area, click **Print Ranges** (located in the Format menu), and then select **Remove**.

Steps for Using the Print Ranges Option:

Step 1: Create a new Calc spreadsheet.

Step 2: Highlight the cells that will be included in the **Print Range**.

Step 3: Click **Format**, located on the Menu Bar.

Step 4: From the Format drop-down menu, click **Print Ranges** and then select **Define**. The print area will be set.

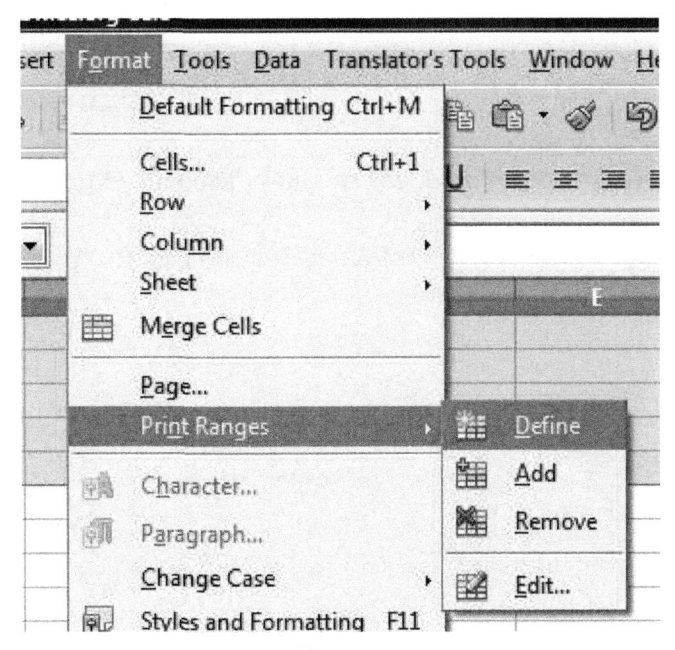

Figure 5

Note – Add more data to the print area by first selecting the desired cells, and then from the Format menu, click **Print Ranges** and then select **Add**. The selected cells will be added to any previously selected data.

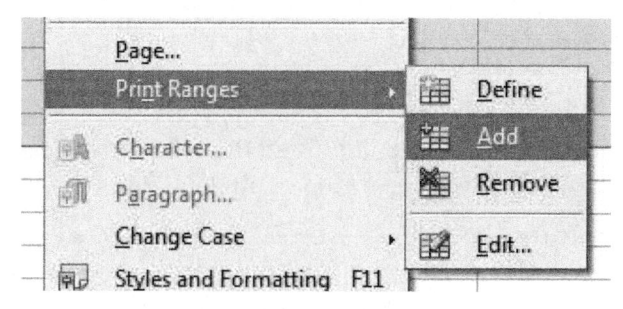

Figure 6

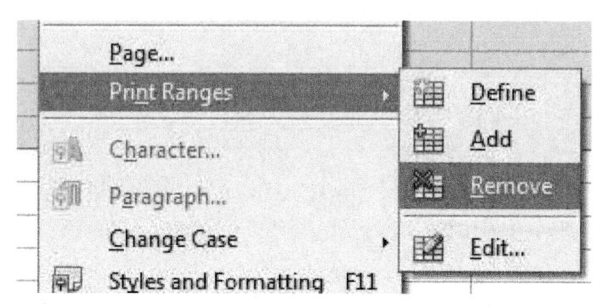

Figure 7

Growth & Assessment

1. What are the two options for specifying a print area?

2. The Shrink button will shrink the **Print Ranges** dialog box.

    a. TRUE

    b. FALSE

3. Where is the **Add** feature found, which allows users to add more data to the print area?

4. **Remove** will clear the print area.

    a. TRUE

    b. FALSE

Section 3.15 – Printing Ranges of Cells

Section Objective:

- Learn how to print ranges of cells.

Printing Ranges of Cells

OpenOffice Calc allows users to manually select contiguous ranges of cells for printing, or select multiple non-contiguous ranges for printing. Both of these options are useful when only certain portions of the spreadsheet need to be printed. The following steps outline how both of these options can be accessed and utilized.

Printing Contiguous Ranges

Step 1: Open a previously saved Calc spreadsheet and highlight a group of cells.

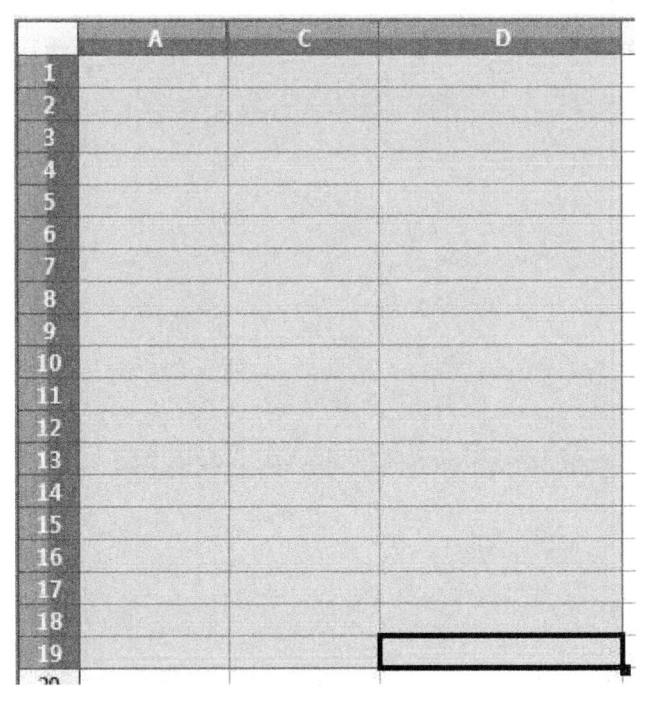

Figure 1

Step 2: Click **File**, located on the Menu Bar.

Step 3: From the File drop-down menu, select **Print**. The **Print** dialog box will appear.

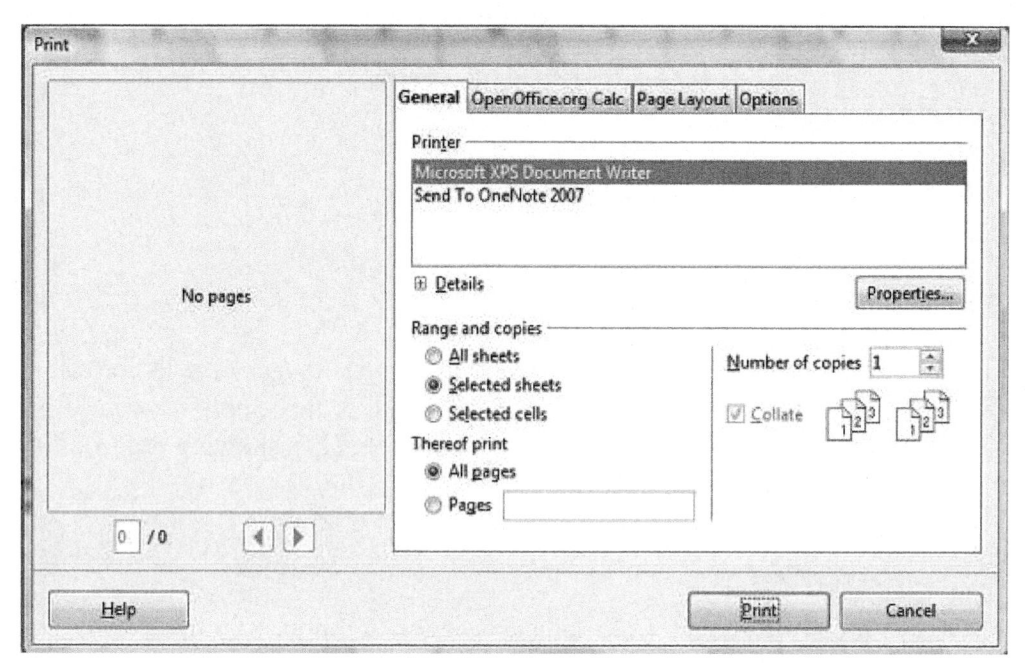

Figure 2

Note – The keyboard shortcut **CTRL + P** will also open the **Print** dialog box.

Step 4: In the **Range and Copies** portion of the dialog box, select **Selected Cells**.

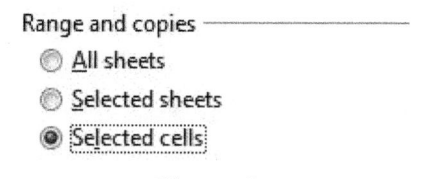

Figure 3

Step 5: Click **OK**. The specified range of cells will be printed.

Printing Non-Contiguous Ranges

Step 1: Open a previously saved Calc spreadsheet and highlight the first range to be printed.

Step 2: Hold the **CTRL** key, and then select the second range to be printed.

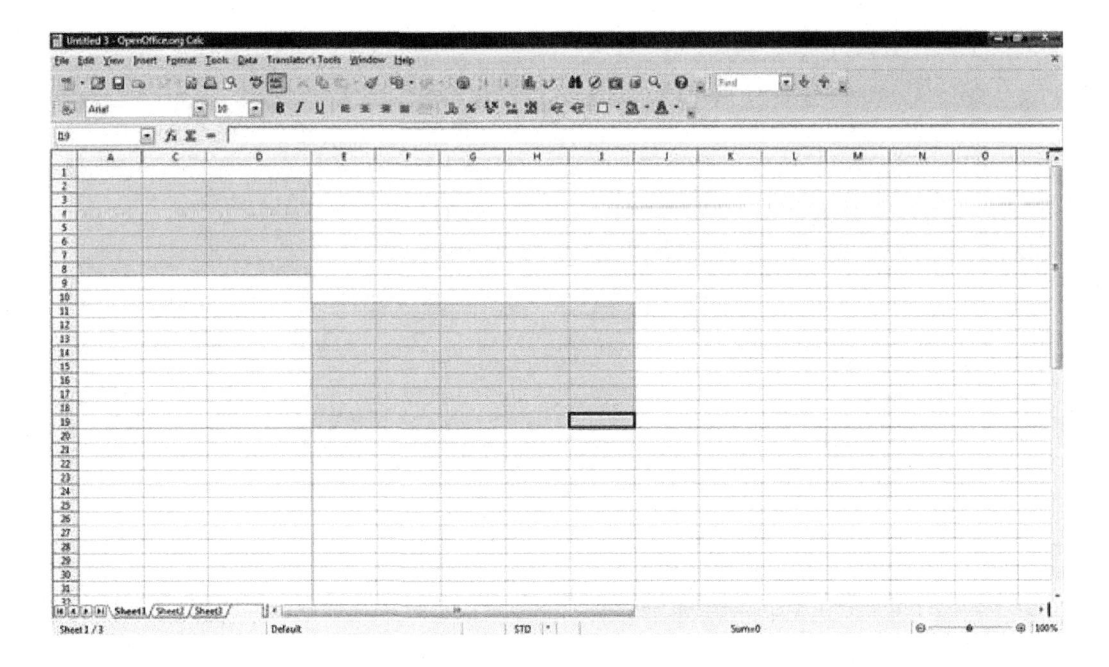

Figure 4

Step 3: For each additional range to be printed, repeat **Step 2**.

Step 4: Click File, located on the Menu Bar.

Step 5: From the File drop-down menu, select **Print**. The **Print** dialog box will appear.

Step 6: In the **Range and Copies** portion of the dialog box, select **Selected Cells**.

Step 7: Click **Print**. The specified ranges of cells will be printed.

Printing Selected Spreadsheets

When working in Calc, users may have multiple sheets in a spreadsheet document and may only want to print certain sheets. Calc allows users to do this by using spreadsheet groups.

Note – This method will print the active area of each sheet.

Step 1: Open a previously saved Calc spreadsheet.

Step 2: Click **File**, located on the Menu Bar.

Step 3: From the File drop-down menu, select **Print**. The **Print** dialog box will appear.

Step 4: Within the **Range and Copies** portion of the dialog box, select **Selected Sheets**.

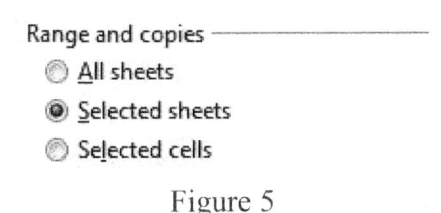

Figure 5

165

Step 5: In the **Thereof Print** section users can either print all sheets of the spreadsheet document, or select specific sheets to print. For this exercise, select Pages.

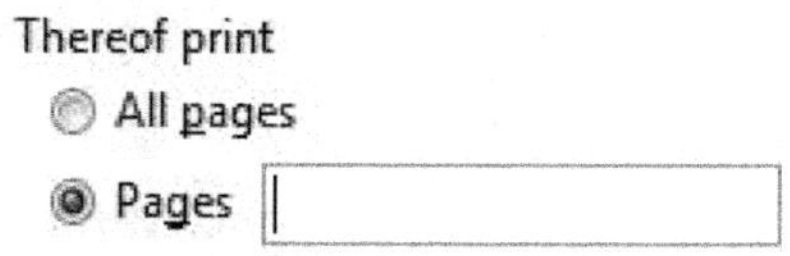

Figure 6

Step 6: In the textbox next to Pages, enter the desired sheet numbers. Do this by adding a comma between the specific sheet numbers. For example, if "**1,3**" was entered into the textbox, sheets 1 and 3 would print.

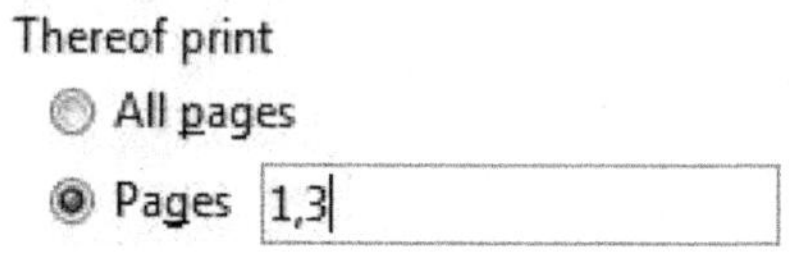

Figure 7

Step 7: Once the desired sheet numbers have been entered into the textbox, click **OK**. The selected sheets will print.

Growth & Assessment

1. What is the keyboard shortcut to open the Print dialog box?

2. Which section allows users to select the sheets printed?

3. Users are able to select the range of cells that will be printed.

   a. TRUE

   b. FALSE

Appendix

OpenOffice Volume II: Calc Unit 1

Section 1.1

1. The intersection of a column and row
2. b. FALSE
3. A single sheet within a spreadsheet document
4. An equal sign (=)

Section 1.2

1. CTRL + N
2. Spreadsheet
3. a. TRUE

Section 1.3

1. .ods
2. a. TRUE
3. CTRL + S
4. The Save As dialog box allows the user to select a particular file format when saving.

Section 1.4

1. Cell Style and Page Style
2. a. TRUE
3. Calc allows the user to modify the font, font size, and typeface of the text entered into the cells.
4. F11

Section 1.5

1. .79 inches
2. Blank borders that go around the outside of the spreadsheet
3. a. TRUE

Section 1.6

1. CTRL + Z
2. a. TRUE
3. While dragging a cell, hold down the CTRL key before letting go of the left mouse button.

Section 1.7

1. The Cut technique moves the data from one cell to a different cell, while deleting the data from the original cell.
2. CTRL + X
3. a. TRUE
4. The drag and drop method

Section 1.8

1. a. TRUE
2. When large amounts of data need to be inserted into a spreadsheet
3. Above the row in which the selected cell is located
4. To the left of the column in which the selected cell is located

Section 1.9

1. b. FALSE
2. b. FALSE
3. Other information within the spreadsheet can cause distractions
4. Numbers

Section 1.10

1. a. TRUE
2. Category
3. ;;;
4. b. FALSE

Section 1.11

1. This feature is very important when the data from one section needs to be referenced or moved to another section within the same spreadsheet.
2. All cells above and to the left of the selected cell will be frozen.
3. a. TRUE

Section 1.12

1. a. TRUE
2. All cells above and to the left of the chosen cell
3. a. TRUE
4. It creates copies of the spreadsheet

Section 1.13

1. Merge Cells and Center
2. CTRL + E
3. a. TRUE
4. The Align Center Horizontally button

Section 1.14

1. a. TRUE
2. Within Gallery
3. Digital images that can be added to a document

Section 1.15

1. Find & Replace
2. CTRL + F
3. The Find All button
4. b. FALSE

OpenOffice Volume II: Calc Unit 2

Section 2.1

1. a. TRUE
2. Perform calculations
3. An Equal Sign "="
4. a. TRUE

Section 2.2

1. Name Box
2. An adjacent group of cells within a spreadsheet
3. a. TRUE
4. In the Define Database Range dialog box

Section 2.3

1. The value or cell reference that will be used to produce the result of the formula
2. A command given to an operand
3. Any number or cell reference: 1, 2, 3… A1, A2, A3…
4. b. FALSE

Section 2.4

1. It connects, or concatenates, two values to produce one continuous text value
2. b. FALSE
3. B21 is less than B4
4. a. TRUE

Section 2.5

1. a. TRUE
2. Precedents and dependents
3. By going through the Tools menu

Section 2.6

1. The formula contains pieces of text that Calc does not recognize; such as an incorrectly named range.

2. a. TRUE

3. Auditing

4. #REF

Section 2.7

1. It allows the user to break down data into subtotals.

2. a. TRUE

3. Any five of the following: Sum, Count, Average, Max, Min, Product, Count (numbers only), StDev (Sample), StDevP (Population), Var (Sample), VarP (Population).

Section 2.8

1. b. FALSE

2. Step 1: Select the chart by clicking the left mouse button. Step 2: Click and hold one of the border corners. Step 3: While holding the left mouse button, drag the mouse to resize the chart and then release the mouse button. The chart will be resized.

3. a. TRUE

Section 2.9

1. a. TRUE

2. By copying the data to multiple spreadsheets, the user can perform different calculations to one set of data without disrupting the original data collected

3. Hold down the CTRL key and click the tabs of the different spreadsheets that the data will be copied into

Section 2.10

1. Generic filters that can be used on any type of data within a column
2. To limit the rows and columns that are visible within the spreadsheet
3. a. TRUE
4. To remove the AutoFilter from the table, click the arrow icon in the filtered column and then select All

Section 2.11

1. b. FALSE
2. It allows the user to filter a range of information and set multiple criteria for the filter
3. b. FALSE
4. Any data that matched a one or more selected criteria would be shown within the spreadsheet

Section 2.12

1. a. TRUE
2. It shrinks the dialog box enough to view the Criteria Matrix
3. AND
4. OR

Section 2.13

1. When trying to access information quickly without having to create formulas
2. Any two of the following: Average, CountA, Count, Maximum, Minimum, Sum, None
3. a. TRUE

Section 2.14

1. a. TRUE
2. Valid entry types
3. a. TRUE

Section 2.15

1. On the Formatting Toolbar
2. Which column the sort will be applied to
3. b. FALSE

OpenOffice Volume II: Calc Unit 3

Section 3.1

1. Any of the three: Italics, underline, bold
2. a. TRUE
3. 409 point

Section 3.2

1. The Currency Button allows the user to change the formatting of the numerical data to the currency data type.
2. a. TRUE
3. b. FALSE
4. Left Justified, Right Justified, Center Justified, and Justified

Section 3.3

1. From the Toolbar and the Format Cells dialog box
2. Font Effects tab
3. Select the Font Color button on the Toolbar

Section 3.4

1. a. TRUE
2. Default Formatting
3. a. TRUE

Section 3.5

1. Using the Fill command
2. Through the Edit menu on the Menu bar
3. Bottom right of the selected cells
4. a. TRUE

Section 3.6

1. Portable Document Format
2. The option to make the exported PDF password protected
3. a. TRUE
4. Which pages to include in the PDF and type of compression to use for images

Section 3.7

1. a. TRUE
2. Decimal places and Leading zeroes
3. Any three of the following: User-define, Number, Percent, Currency, Date, Time, Scientific, Fraction, Boolean Value, Text

Section 3.8

1. =now()
2. =today()
3. b. FALSE
4. The current date will appear in the selected cell and will stay the same regardless of other actions taken in the application.

Section 3.9

1. Above the cells at the top of a spreadsheet
2. b. FALSE
3. Adds a Date place holder to the Header/Footer.
4. Opens up the Font dialog box. From here the user can change the formatting of characters used in the Header/Footer

Section 3.10

1. a. TRUE
2. Cell style
3. a. TRUE

Section 3.11

1. a. TRUE
2. The Alignment tab allows the user to choose where the data will be located within the cell.
3. The Background tab allows the user to select a background color for the cells that meet the specified criteria.

Section 3.12

1. a. TRUE
2. Within the Cell Style dialog box
3. a. TRUE
4. Any two of the following: Organizer, Numbers, Font, Font Effect, Alignment, Borders, Background, Cell Protection

Section 3.13

1. Portrait
2. a. TRUE
3. Landscape
4. 11"

Section 3.14

1. Edit Print Ranges dialog box and the Print Ranges option
2. a. TRUE
3. Within the Print Ranges option through the Format menu
4. a. TRUE

Section 3.15

1. CTRL + P
2. Thereof Print
3. a. TRUE

Printed in Great Britain
by Amazon